An American National Standard

IEEE Standards for
Local Area Networks:

Carrier Sense Multiple Access with Collision Detection (CSMA/CD) Access Method and Physical Layer Specifications

Published by
The Institute of Electrical and Electronics Engineers, Inc

Distributed in cooperation with
Wiley-Interscience, a division of John Wiley & Sons, Inc

ANSI/IEEE
Std 802.3-1985

IEEE Standards for Local Area Networks:

Carrier Sense Multiple Access with Collision Detection (CSMA/CD) Access Method and Physical Layer Specifications

Sponsor

**Technical Committee on Computer Communications
of the
IEEE Computer Society**

This standard has been adopted for U.S. federal government use.

Details concerning its use within the federal government are contained in FIPS PUB 107, Local Area Networks: Base Band Carrier Sense Multiple Access with Collision Detection Access Method and Physical Layer Specifications and Link Layer Protocol. For a complete list of the publications available in the FEDERAL INFORMATION PROCESSING STANDARDS Series, write to the Standards Processing Coordinator, Institute for Computer Sciences and Technology, National Bureau of Standards, Gaithersburg, MD 20899, U.S.A.

ISBN 0-471-82749-5

Library of Congress Catalog Number 84-43096

December 31, 1984   *SH09738*

Foreword

(This Foreword is not a part of IEEE Std 802.3-1985, Carrier Sense Multiple Access with Collision Detection (CSMA/CD) Access Method and Physical Layer Specifications.)

This standard is part of a family of standards for Local Area Networks (LANs). The relationship between this standard and other members of the family is shown below. (The numbers in the figure refer to IEEE standard numbers.)

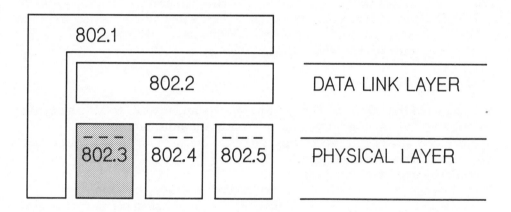

This family of standards deals with the Physical and Data Link Layers as defined by the ISO Open System Interconnection Reference Model. The access standards define three types of media access technologies and associated physical media, each appropriate for particular applications or system objectives. The standards defining these technologies are

(1) IEEE Std 802.3-1985 (ISO DIS 8802/3), a bus utilizing CSMA/CD as the access method

(2) IEEE Std 802.4-1985 (ISO DIS 8802/4), a bus utilizing token passing as the access method

(3) IEEE Std 802.5-1985 (ISO DP 8802/5), a ring utilizing token passing as the access method

Other access methods (for example, metropolitan area networks) are under investigation. IEEE Std 802.2-1985 (ISO DIS 8802/2), the Logical Link Control standard, is used in conjunction with the medium access standards.

IEEE P802.1 describes the relationship among these standards and their relationship to the ISO Open System Interconnection Reference Model in more detail. This companion document also will contain networking management standards and information on internetworking. The reader of this standard is urged to become familiar with the complete family of standards.

The local area network access mechanism specified by this standard may include patented matter. The IEEE Standards Office calls attention to the fact that it is claimed that the process of the local area network access mechanism described throughout this standard is the subject of United States patent numbers 4 063 220 and 4 099 024 and corresponding patent of foreign countries owned by the Xerox Corporation. Although these patents appear to cover the access mechanism subject in this standard, the IEEE takes no position with respect to patent validity. The Xerox Corporation has assured the IEEE that it is willing to grant a license under these patents on reasonable and nondiscriminatory terms and conditions to anyone wishing to obtain such a license. The Xerox Corporation's undertakings in this respect are on file with the IEEE Standards Office and the license details may be obtained from the Office of General Counsel of Xerox Corporation, whose address is PO Box 1600, Stamford, CT 06904, USA.

ISO Standard

Portions of the text of this standard are the standard ISO 8802/3, supported by the ISO, International Organization for Standardization.

Some portions of the text of this standard are peculiar to IEEE Std 802.4-1984, specifically areas relating to

(1) References to national standards

(2) Recommendations and guidelines related to safety concerns

To avoid duplications of standards the ISO has not developed a separate international standard. Those sections of this standard that are not part of the International Standard are prefaced with a note enclosed in braces "{...}".

At the time this text was printed, ISO Standard 8802/2 was a Draft International Standard (DIS).

IEEE Std 802.3-1985

The first edition of the standard defines a 10 Mb/s baseband implementation of the Physical Layer using the CSMA/CD access method. It is anticipated that future editions of the standard may provide additional implementations of the physical layer to support different needs (for example, media, and data rates).

This standard contains state-of-the-art material. The area covered by this standard is undergoing evolution. Revisions are anticipated to this standard within the next few years to clarify existing material, to correct possible errors, and to incorporate new related material.

Readers wishing to know the state of revisions should contact the 802.3 Working Group Chairman through

Secretary,
IEEE Standards Board
Institute of Electrical and Electronics Engineers, Inc
345 East 47th Street
New York, NY 10017 USA

The IEEE 802.3 Working Group that developed this standard had the following membership during the ballot cycle:

Donald C. Loughry, *Chairman*

Individuals who contributed actively in the development of this standard throughout its elaboration were:

The ECMA TC24 Committee on Communication Protocols also provided helpful input in the development of this standard.

The IEEE 802.3 Working Group acknowledges and appreciates that many concepts embodied in this standard are based largely upon the CSMA/CD access method earlier described in *The Ethernet* specification as written jointly by individuals from Xerox Corporation, Digital Equipment Corporation, and Intel Corporation. Appreciation is also expressed to Robert M. Metcalf and David R. Boggs for their pioneering work in establishing the original concepts.

When the IEEE Standards Board approved this standard on June 23, 1983, it had the following membership:

James H. Beall, *Chairman*   **Edward Chelotti,** *Vice Chairman*

Sava I. Sherr, *Secretary*

Contents

An American National Standard
IEEE Standards for Local Area Networks:

Carrier Sense Multiple Access with Collision Detection (CSMA/CD) Access Method and Physical Layer Specifications

1. Introduction

1.1 Overview

1.1.1 Basic Concepts. The Carrier Sense Multiple Access with Collision Detection (CSMA/CD) media access method is the means by which two or more stations share a common bus transmission medium. To transmit, a station waits (defers) for a quiet period on the medium (that is, no other station is transmitting) and then sends the intended message in bit-serial form. If, after initiating a transmission, the message collides with that of another station, then each transmitting station intentionally sends a few additional bytes to ensure propagation of the collision throughout the system. The station remains silent for a random amount of time (backoff) before attempting to transmit again. Each aspect of this access method process is specified in detail in subsequent sections of this standard.

This is a comprehensive standard for Local Area Networks employing CSMA/CD as the access method. This standard is intended to encompass several media types and techniques for signal rates from 1 Mb/s to 20 Mb/s. This edition of the standard provides the necessary specification and related parameter values for a 10 Mb/s baseband implementation. It is expected that subsequent editions of this standard will provide similar specifications for additional implementations (for example, other data rates and physical media).

1.1.2 Architectural Perspectives. There are two important ways to view local area network design corresponding to

(1) Architecture, emphasizing the logical divisions of the system and how they fit together

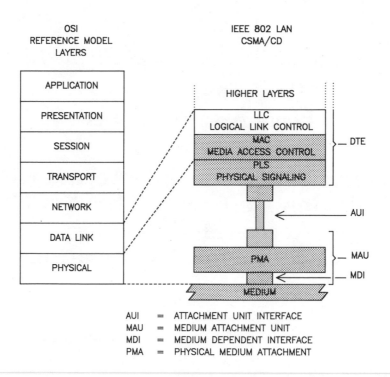

Fig 1-1
LAN Standard Relationship to the
OSI Reference Model

(2) Implementation, emphasizing actual components, their packaging and interconnection

This standard is organized along architectural lines, emphasizing the large-scale separation of the system into two parts: the Media Access Control (MAC) sublayer of the Data Link Layer, and the Physical Layer. These layers are intended to correspond closely to the lowest layers of the ISO Model for Open Systems Interconnection (see Fig 1-1). The Logical Link Control (LLC) sublayer and MAC sublayer together encompass the functions intended for the Data Link Layer as defined in the OSI model.

1.1.2.1 An architectural organization of the standard has two main advantages

(1) *Clarity*. A clean overall division of the design along architectural lines makes the standard clearer

(2) *Flexibility*. Segregation of medium-dependent aspects in the Physical Layer allows the LLC and MAC sublayers to apply to a family of transmission media

Partitioning the Data Link Layer allows various media access methods within the IEEE 802 family of Local Area Network standards.

The architectural model is based on a set of interfaces that may be different from those emphasized in implementations. One critical aspect of the design however shall be addressed largely in terms of the implementation interfaces: compatibility.

1.1.2.2 Two important compatibility interfaces are defined within what is architecturally the Physical Layer.

(1) *Medium Dependent Interface (MDI).* To communicate in a compatible manner, all stations shall adhere rigidly to the exact specification of physical media signals defined in Section 8 (and beyond) in this standard, and to the procedures that define correct behavior of a station. The medium-independent aspects of the LLC sublayer and the MAC sublayer should not be taken as detracting from this point; communication by way of the IEEE 802.3 Local Area Network requires complete compatibility at the Physical Medium interface (that is, the coaxial cable interface).

(2) *Attachment Unit Interface (AUI).* It is anticipated that most stations will be located some distance from their connection to the coaxial cable. A small amount of circuitry will exist in the Medium Attachment Unit (MAU) directly adjacent to the coaxial cable, while the majority of the hardware and all of the software will be placed within the station. The AUI is defined as a second compatibility interface. While conformance with this interface is not strictly necessary to ensure communication, it is highly recommended, since it allows maximum flexibility in intermixing MAUs and stations.

1.1.3 Layer Interfaces. In the architectural model used here, the layers interact by way of well defined interfaces, providing services as specified in Section 2. In general, the interface requirements are as follows:

(1) The interface between the MAC sublayer and the LLC sublayer includes facilities for transmitting and receiving frames, and provides per-operation status information for use by higher-level error recovery procedures.

(2) The interface between the MAC sublayer and the Physical Layer includes signals for framing (carrier sense, transmit initiation) and contention resolution (collision detect), facilities for passing a pair of serial bit streams (transmit, receive) between the two layers, and a wait function for timing.

These interfaces are described more precisely in 4.3. Additional interfaces are necessary to allow higher level network-management facilities to interact with these layers to perform operation, maintenance, and planning functions. Network-management functions will be discussed in Section 5.

1.1.4 Application Areas. The applications environment for the Local Area Network is intended to be commercial and light industrial. Use of CSMA/CD LANs in home or heavy industrial environments, while not precluded, is not considered within the scope of this standard.

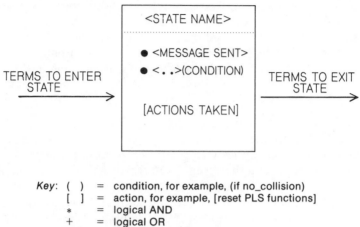

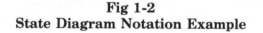

Key: ( ) = condition, for example, (if no_collision)
      [ ] = action, for example, [reset PLS functions]
      *   = logical AND
      +   = logical OR
      Tw   = Wait Time, implementation dependent
      Td   = Delay Timeout
      Tb   = Backoff Timeout
      UCT = unconditional transition

Fig 1-2
State Diagram Notation Example

1.2 Notation

1.2.1 State Diagram Conventions. The operation of a protocol can be described by subdividing the protocol into a number of interrelated functions. The operation of the functions can be described by state diagrams. Each diagram represents the domain of a function and consists of a group of connected, mutually exclusive states. Only one state of a function is active at any given time (see Fig 1-2).

Each state that the function can assume is represented by a rectangle. These are divided into two parts by a horizontal line. In the upper part the state is identified by a name. The lower part contains the name of any ON signal that is generated by the function.

All permissible transitions between the states of a function are represented graphically by arrows between them. A transition that is global in nature (that is, exit condition from all states to the IDLE or RESET state) is indicated by an open arrow.

1.2.2 Service Specification Method and Notation. The service of a layer or sublayer is the set of capabilities that it offers to a user in the next higher (sub)layer. Abstract services are specified here by describing the service primitives and parameters which characterize each service. This definition of service is independent of any particular implementation (see Fig 1-3).

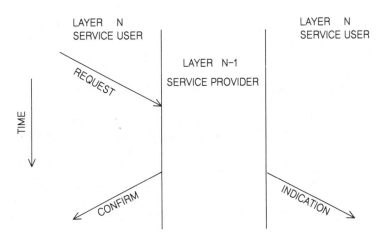

Fig 1-3
Service Primitive Notation

Specific implementations may also include provisions for interface inter-actions that have no direct end-to-end effects. Examples of such local inter-actions include interface flow control, status requests and indications, error notifications, and layer management. Specific implementation details are omitted from this service specification because they will differ from imple-mentation to implementation and because they do not impact the peer-to-peer protocols.

1.2.2.1 Classification of Service Primitives. Primitives are of three generic types:

(1) REQUEST. The request primitive is passed from layer N to layer N-1 to request that a service be initiated.

(2) INDICATION. The indication primitive is passed from layer N-1 to layer N to indicate an internal layer N-1 event that is significant to layer N. This event may be logically related to a remote service request, or may be caused by an event internal to layer N-1.

(3) CONFIRM. The confirm primitive is passed from layer N-1 to layer N to convey the results of the associated previous service request.

The service primitives are an abstraction of the functional specification and the user-layer interaction. The abstract definition does not contain local detail of the user/provider interaction. For instance, it does not indicate the local mechanism that allows a user to indicate that it is awaiting an incoming call. Each primitive has a set of zero or more parameters, representing data ele-ments that shall be passed to qualify the functions invoked by the primitive. Parameters indicate information available in a user/provider interaction; in any particular interface, some parameters may be explicitly stated (even though not explicitly defined in the primitive) or implicitly associated with the service access point. Similarly, in any particular protocol specification, functions corresponding to a service primitive may be explicitly defined or implicitly available.

1.2.3 Physical Layer and Media Notation. Users of this standard need to reference which particular implementation is being used or identified. Therefore, a means of identifying each implementation is given by a simple, three-field, type notation that is explicitly stated at the beginning of each relevant section. In general, the Physical Layer type is specified by these fields;

<data rate in Mb/s> <medium type> <maximum segment length (· 100 m)>

For example, the standard contains a 10 Mb/s baseband specification identified as; "TYPE 10BASE5", meaning a 10 Mb/s baseband medium whose maximum segment length is 500 m. Each successive Physical Layer specification will state its own unique TYPE identifier along similar lines.

1.2.4 Physical Layer Message Notation. Messages generated within the Physical Layer, either within or between, PLS and the MAU are designated by italic type to designate either form of physical or logical message used to execute the physical layer signaling process (for example, *input_idle* or *mau_available*).

1.3 References

When the following standards referred to in this standard are superseded by an approved revision the latest revision shall apply.

References to ANSI, EIA, IEEE, MIL, and NFPA standards are not part of the equivalent ISO standard.

[1] ANSI/EIA RS-364-1971 (R 1976), Standard Test Procedures for Low-Frequency (Below 3 MHz) Electrical Connectors.[1]

[2] ANSI/IEEE Std 770X3.97-1983, IEEE Standard Pascal Computer Programming Language.

[3] ANSI/NFPA 70-1984, National Electrical Code.[2]

[4] EIA CB8-1981, Components Bulletin (Cat 4) List of Approved Agencies, US and Other Countries, Impacting Electronic Components and Equipment (August).[3]

---

[1] ANSI publications are available from the Sales Department, American National Standards Institute, 1430 Broadway, New York, NY 10018.

[2] The National Electrical Code is published by the National Fire Protection Association, Batterymarch Park, Quincy, MA 02269. Copies are also available from the Sales Department, American National Standards Institute, 1430 Broadway, New York, NY 10018.

[3] EIA publications are available from Electronic Industries Association, 2001 Eye Street, NW Washington, DC 20006.

[5] MIL-C-17-1964, Cables, Radio Frequency, Coaxial, Dual Coaxial, Twin Conductor, and Twin Lead — Characteristic Impedance.[4]

[6] MIL-C-24308-1972, Rack and Panel General Specifications for Connector, Electric, Rectangular, Miniature Polarized Shell.

[7] BRINCH HANSEN, P. *The Architecture of Concurrent Programs.* Englewood Cliffs, NJ: Prentice Hall, 1977.

[8] FCC Docket 20780-1980 [Part 15], Technical Standards for Computing Equipment. Amendment of Part 15 to redefine and clarify the rules governing restricted radiation devices and low-power communication devices. Reconsidered First Report and Order, April 1980.[5]

[9] HAMMOND, J.L., BROWN, J.E., and LIU, S.S. Development of a Transmission Error Model and and Error Control Model. *Technical Report RADC-TR-75-138.* Rome: Air Development Center, (1975).

[10] UL Subject no 758: UL VW-1, Description of Appliance Wiring Material.[6]

---

[4] MIL publications are available from Superintendent of Documents, US Government Printing Office, Washington, DC 20402.

[5] FCC publications are available from the Federal Communications Commission, Washington, DC 20402.

[6] UL publications are available from Underwriters Laboratories, Inc., 1285 Walt Whitman Road, Melville, New York 11747.

2. MAC Service Specification

2.1 Scope and Field of Application. This section specifies the services provided by the Media Access Control (MAC) sublayer to the Logical Link Control (LLC) sublayer for the IEEE 802 Local Area Network Standard (see Fig 2-1). The services are described in an abstract way and do not imply any

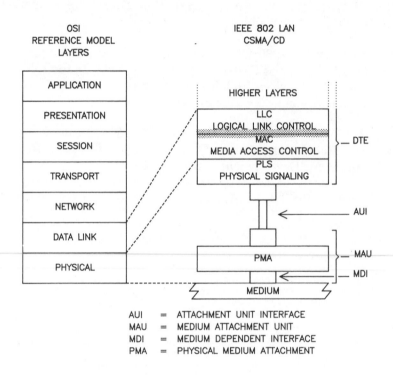

OSI
REFERENCE MODEL
LAYERS

IEEE 802 LAN
CSMA/CD

APPLICATION

HIGHER LAYERS

PRESENTATION

LLC
LOGICAL LINK CONTROL

SESSION

MAC
MEDIA ACCESS CONTROL

TRANSPORT

PLS
PHYSICAL SIGNALING

NETWORK

DATA LINK

PHYSICAL

PMA

MEDIUM

_ DTE

_ AUI

_ MAU
_ MDI

AUI = ATTACHMENT UNIT INTERFACE
MAU = MEDIUM ATTACHMENT UNIT
MDI = MEDIUM DEPENDENT INTERFACE
PMA = PHYSICAL MEDIUM ATTACHMENT

Fig 2-1
Service Specification Relation to the LAN Model

particular implementation, or any exposed interface. There is not necessarily a one-to-one correspondence between the primitives and the formal procedures and interfaces described in 4.2 and 4.3.

2.2 Overview of the Service

2.2.1 General Description of Services Provided by the Layer. The services provided by the MAC sublayer allow the local LLC sublayer entity to exchange LLC data units with peer LLC sublayer entities. Optional support may be provided for resetting the MAC sublayer entity to a known state.

2.2.2 Model Used for the Service Specification. The model used in this service specification is identical to that used in 1.2.

2.2.3 Overview of Interactions

MA_DATA.request
MA_DATA.confirm
MA_DATA.indication

2.2.4 Basic Services and Options. The MA_DATA.request, MA_DATA.confirm, and MA_DATA.indication service primitives described in this section are considered mandatory.

2.3 Detailed Service Specification

2.3.1 MA_DATA.request

2.3.1.1 Function. This primitive defines the transfer of data from a local LLC sublayer entity to a single peer LLC entity or multiple peer LLC entities in the case of group addresses.

2.3.1.2 Semantics of the Service Primitive. The semantics of the primitive are as follows:

```
MA_DATA.request     (
                    destination_address,
                    m_sdu,
                    service_class
                    )
```

The destination address parameter may specify either an individual or a group MAC entity address. It shall contain sufficient information to create the DA field that is appended to the frame by the local MAC sublayer entity and any lower level address information. The m_sdu parameter specifies the MAC service data unit to be transmitted by the MAC sublayer entity. There is sufficient information associated with m_sdu for the MAC sublayer entity to determine the length of the data unit. The service_class parameter indicates a quality of service requested by LLC or higher layer (see 2.3.1.5).

2.3.1.3 When Generated. This primitive is generated by the LLC sublayer entity whenever data shall be transferred to a peer LLC entity or entities. This can be in response to a request from higher layers of protocol or from data generated internally to the LLC sublayer, such as required by Type 2 service.

2.3.1.4 Effect of Receipt. The receipt of this primitive will cause the MAC entity to append all MAC specific fields, including DA, SA, and any fields that are unique to the particular media access method, and pass the properly formed frame to the lower layers of protocol for transfer to the peer MAC sublayer entity or entities.

2.3.1.5 Additional Comments. The CSMA/CD MAC protocol provides a single quality of service regardless of the service_class requested.

2.3.2 MA_DATA.confirm

2.3.2.1 Function. This primitive has local significance and shall provide an appropriate response to the LLC sublayer MA_DATA.request primitive signifying the success or failure of the request.

2.3.2.2 Semantics of the Service Primitive. The semantics of this primitive are as follows:

MA_DATA.confirm (transmission_status)

The transmission_status parameter is used to pass status information back to the local requesting LLC sublayer entity. It is used to indicate the success or failure (for example, excessive collisions) of the previous associated MA_DATA.request.

2.3.2.3 When Generated. This primitive is generated in response to an MA_DATA.request from the local LLC sublayer entity.

2.3.2.4 Effect of Receipt. The effect of receipt of this primitive by the LLC sublayer is unspecified.

2.3.2.5 Additional Comments. It is assumed that sufficient information is available to the LLC sublayer to associate the response with the appropriate request (for example, the association may be implied by the order of the responses, since the MAC sublayer requires that the requests be serviced in a first-in-first-out manner).

2.3.3 MA_DATA.indication

2.3.3.1 Function. This primitive defines the transfer of data from the MAC sublayer entity to the LLC sublayer entity or entities in the case of group addresses.

2.3.3.2 Semantics of the Service Primitive. The semantics of the primitive are as follows:

MA_DATA.indication   (
                      destination_address,
                      source_address,
                      m_sdu,
                      reception_status
)

The destination_address parameter may be either an individual or a group address as specified by the DA field of the incoming frame. The source_address parameter is an individual address as specified by the SA field of the incoming frame. The m_sdu parameter specifies the MAC service data unit as received by the local MAC entity. The reception_status parameter is used to pass status information to the peer LLC sublayer entity.

2.3.3.3 When Generated. The MA_DATA.indication is passed from the MAC sublayer entity to the LLC sublayer entity or entities to indicate the arrival of a frame to the local MAC sublayer entity. Such frames are reported only if they are validly formed, received without error, and their destination address designates the local MAC entity.

2.3.3.4 Effect of Receipt. The effect of receipt of this primitive by the LLC sublayer is unspecified.

2.3.3.5 Additional Comments. If the local MAC sublayer entity is designated by the destination_address parameter of an MA_DATA.request, the indication primitive will also be invoked by the MAC entity to the local LLC entity. This full duplex characteristic of the MAC sublayer may be due to unique functionality within the MAC sublayer or full duplex characteristics of the lower layers (for example, all frames transmitted to the broadcast address will invoke MA_DATA.indication at all stations in the network including the station that generated the request).

3. Media Access Control Frame Structure

3.1 Overview. This section defines in detail the frame structure for data-communication systems using local area network MAC procedures. It defines the relative positions of the various components of the MAC frame. It defines the method for representing station addresses. It defines a partition of the address space into individual (single station) and group (multicast or multi-station) addresses, and into user administered and globally administered addresses.

3.1.1 MAC Frame Format. Figure 3-1 shows the eight fields of a frame: the preamble, Start Frame Delimiter, the addresses of the frame's source and destination, a length field to indicate the length of the following field containing the LLC data to be transmitted, a field that contains padding if required, and the frame check sequence field containing a cyclic redundancy check value to detect errors in received frames. Of these eight fields, all are of fixed size except the LLC data and PAD fields, which may contain any integer number of octets between the minimum and maximum values determined by the specific implementation of the CSMA/CD Media Access mechanism. See 4.4 for particular implementations.

The minimum and maximum frame size limits in 4.4 refer to that portion of the frame from the destination address field through the frame check sequence field, inclusive.

Relative to Fig 3-1, the octets of a frame are transmitted from top to bottom, and the bits of each octet are transmitted from left to right.

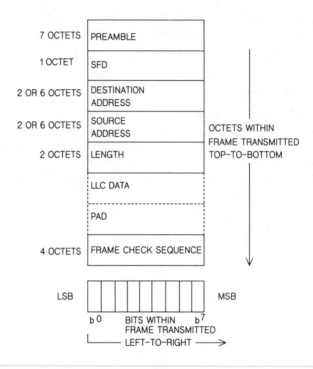

Fig 3-1
MAC Frame Format

3.2. Elements of the MAC Frame

3.2.1 Preamble Field. The preamble field is a 7-octet field that is used to allow the PLS circuitry to reach its steady-state synchronization with the received frame timing (see 4.2.5).

3.2.2 Start Frame Delimiter Field. The Start Frame Delimiter (SFD) field is the sequence 10101011. It immediately follows the preamble pattern and indicates the start of a frame.

3.2.3 Address Fields. Each MAC frame shall contain two address fields: the Destination Address field and the Source Address field, in that order. The Destination Address field shall specify the destination addressee(s) for which the frame is intended. The Source Address field shall identify the station from which the frame was initiated. The representation of each address field shall be as follows (see Fig 3-2):

(1) Each address field shall contain either 16 bits or 48 bits. However, at any given time, the Source and Destination Address size shall be the same for all stations on a particular local area network.

48 BIT ADDRESS FORMAT

16 BIT ADDRESS FORMAT

```
I/G  = 0   INDIVIDUAL ADDRESS
I/G  = 1   GROUP ADDRESS
U/L  = 0   GLOBALLY ADMINISTERED ADDRESS
U/L  = 1   LOCALLY ADMINISTERED ADDRESS
```

Fig 3-2
Address Field Format

(2) The support of 16 bit or 48 bit address length for Source and Destination Address shall be left to the manufacturer as an implementation decision. There is no requirement that manufacturers support both sizes.

(3) The first bit (LSB) shall be used in the Destination Address field as an address type designation bit to identify the Destination Address either as an individual or as a group address. In the Source Address field, the first bit is reserved and set to 0 . If this bit is 0 , it shall indicate that the address field contains an individual address. If this bit is 1 , it shall indicate that the address field contains a group address that identifies none, one or more, or all of the stations connected to the local area network.

(4) For 48 bit addresses, the second bit shall be used to distinguish between locally or globally administered addresses. For globally administered (or U, universal) addresses, the bit is set to 0 . If an address is to be assigned locally, this bit shall be set to 1 . Note that for the broadcast address, this bit is also a 1 .

(5) Each octet of each address field shall be transmitted least significant bit first.

3.2.3.1 Address Designation. A MAC sublayer address is of one of two types

(1) *Individual Address.* The address associated with a particular station on the network

(2) *Group Address.* A multi-destination address, associated with one or more stations on a given network. There are two kinds of multicast address:

(a) *Multicast-Group Address.* An address associated by higher-level convention with a group of logically related stations

(b) *Broadcast Address.* A distinguished, predefined multicast address that always denotes the set of all stations on a given local area network

All 1s in the Destination Address field (for 16 bit or 48 bit address size LANs) shall be predefined to be the Broadcast address. This group shall be predefined for each communication medium to consist of all stations actively connected to that medium; it shall be used to broadcast to all the active stations on that medium. All stations shall be able to recognize the Broadcast address. It is not necessary that a station be capable of generating the Broadcast address.

The address space shall also be partitioned into locally administered and globally administered addresses. The nature of a body and the procedures by which it administers these global (U) addresses is beyond the scope of this standard.[7]

3.2.4 Destination Address Field. The Destination Address field specifies the station(s) for which the frame is intended. It may be an individual or multicast (including broadcast) address.

3.2.5 Source Address Field. The Source Address field specifies the station sending the frame. The Source Address field is not interpreted by the CSMA/CD MAC sublayer.

3.2.6 Length Field. The length field is a 2-octet field whose value* indicates the number of LLC data octets in the data field. If the value is less than the minimum required for proper operation of the protocol, a PAD field (a sequence of octets) will be added at the end of the data field but prior to the FCS field, specified below. The procedure that determines the size of the pad field is specified in 4.2.8. The length field is transmitted and received with the high order octet first.

3.2.7 Data and PAD Fields. The data field contains a sequence of n octets. Full data transparency is provided in the sense that any arbitrary sequence of octet values may appear in the data field up to a maximum number specified by the implementation of this standard that is used. A minimum frame size is required for correct CSMA/CD protocol operation and is specified by the particular implementation of the standard. If necessary, the data field is extended by appending extra bits (that is, a pad) in units of octets after the LLC data field but prior to calculating and appending the FCS. The size of the pad, if any, is determined by the size of the data field supplied by LLC and the minimum frame size and address size parameters of the particular implementation. The maximum size of the data field is determined by the maximum frame size and address size parameters of the particular implementation.

---

[7] For information on global (U) address administration contact the Secretary, IEEE Standards Board, 345 East 47 Street, New York, NY 10017.

* Packets with a length field value greater than those specified in 4.4.2 may be ignored, discarded, or used in a private manner. The use of such packets is beyond the scope of this standard.

The length of the PAD field required for LLC data that is n octets long is max $(0, minFrameSize - (8 \cdot n + 2 \cdot addressSize + 48))$ bits. The maximum possible size of the LLC data field is $maxFrameSize - (2 \cdot addressSize + 48)/8$ octets. See 4.4 for a discussion of implementation parameters; see 4.2.3.3 for a discussion of the minFrameSize.

3.2.8 Frame Check Sequence Field. A cyclic redundancy check (CRC) is used by the transmit and receive algorithms to generate a CRC value for the FCS field. The frame check sequence (FCS) field contains a 4-octet (32-bit) cyclic redundancy check (CRC) value. This value is computed as a function of the contents of the source/address, destination/address, length, LLC data, and pad (that is, all fields except the preamble, SFD, and FCS). The encoding is defined by the following generating polynomial.

$$G(x) = x^{32} + x^{26} + x^{23} + x^{22} + x^{16} + x^{12} + x^{11} + x^{10} + x^8 + x^7 + x^5 + x^4 + x^2 + x + 1$$

See reference [9][8] where the symbol n represents an exponent.

Mathematically, the CRC value corresponding to a given frame is defined by the following procedure:

(1) The first 32 bits of the frame are complemented.

(2) The n bits of the frame are then considered to be the coefficients of a polynomial $M(x)$ of degree n-1. (The first bit of the destination address field corresponds to the $x^{(n-1)}$ term and the last bit of the data field corresponds to the x^0 term.)

(3) $M(x)$ is multiplied by x^{32} and divided by $G(x)$, producing a remainder $R(x)$ of degree < 31.

(4) The coefficients of $R(x)$ are considered to be a 32-bit sequence.

(5) The bit sequence is complemented and the result is the CRC.

The 32 bits of the CRC value are placed in the frame check sequence field so that the x^{31} term is the leftmost bit of the first octet, and the x^0 term is the rightmost bit of the last octet. (The bits of the CRC are thus transmitted in the order $x^{31}, x^{30}, \ldots, x^1, x^0$.)

3.3 Order of Bit Transmission. Each octet of the MAC frame, with the exception of the FCS, is transmitted low-order bit first.

3.4. Invalid MAC Frame. An invalid MAC frame shall be defined as one which meets at least one of the following conditions:

(1) The frame length is inconsistent with the length field

(2) It is not an integral number of octets in length

(3) The bits of the incoming frame (exclusive of the FCS field itself) do not generate a CRC value identical to the one received

The contents of invalid MAC frames shall not be passed to LLC. The occurrence of invalid MAC frames may be communicated to network management.

---

[8] The numbers in brackets correspond to those of the references in 1.3.

4. Media Access Control

4.1 Functional Model of the Media Access Control Method

4.1.1 Overview.
The architectural model described in Section 1 is used in this section to provide a functional description of the Local Area Network CSMA/CD MAC sublayer.

The MAC sublayer defines a medium-independent facility, built on the medium-dependent physical facility provided by the Physical Layer, and under the access-layer-independent local area network LLC sublayer. It is applicable to a general class of local area broadcast media suitable for use with the media access discipline known as Carrier Sense Multiple Access with Collision Detection (CSMA/CD).

The LLC sublayer and the MAC sublayer together are intended to have the same function as that described in the OSI model for the Data Link Layer alone. In a broadcast network, the notion of a data link between two network entities does not correspond directly to a distinct physical connection. Nevertheless, the partitioning of functions presented in this standard requires two main functions generally associated with a data link control procedure to be performed in the MAC sublayer. They are

(1) Data encapsulation (transmit and receive)
    (a) Framing (frame boundary delimitation, frame synchronization)
    (b) Addressing (handling of source and destination addresses)
    (c) Error detection (detection of physical medium transmission errors)
(2) Media access management
    (a) Medium allocation (collision avoidance)
    (b) Contention resolution (collision handling)

The remainder of this section provides a functional model of the CSMA/CD MAC method.

4.1.2 IEEE 802 CSMA/CD Operation.
This section provides an overview of frame transmission and reception in terms of the functional model of the architecture. This overview is descriptive, rather than definitional; the formal specifications of the operations described here are given in 4.2 and 4.3. Specific implementations for CSMA/CD mechanisms that meet this standard are given in 4.4. Figure 4-1 provides the architectural model described functionally in the sections below.

The Physical Layer Signaling (PLS) component of the Physical Layer provides an interface to the MAC sublayer for the serial transmission of bits onto the physical media. For completeness, in the operational description below, some of these functions are included as descriptive material. The concise specification of these functions is given in 4.2 for the MAC functions and in Section 7 for PLS.

Transmit frame operations are independent from the receive frame operations. A transmitted frame addressed to the originating station will be received and passed to the LLC sublayer at that station. This characteristic of the

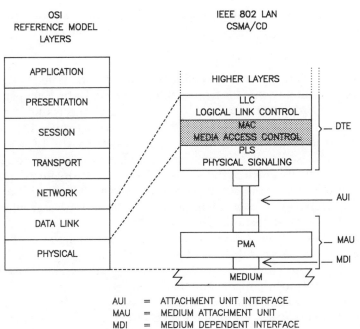

Fig 4-1
MAC Sublayer Partitioning, Relationship to
OSI Reference Model

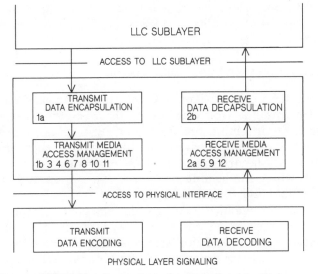

NOTE: Numbers refer to functions listed in 4.1.4.

Fig 4-2
CSMA/CD Media Access Control Functions

MAC sublayer may be implemented by functionality within the MAC sublayer or full duplex characteristics of portions of the lower layers.

4.1.2.1 Normal Operation
4.1.2.1.1 Transmission Without Contention.
When a LLC sublayer requests the transmission of a frame, the Transmit Data Encapsulation component of the CSMA/CD MAC sublayer constructs the frame from the LLC-supplied data. It appends a preamble and a Start Frame Delimiter to the beginning of the frame. Using information passed by the LLC sublayer, the CSMA/CD MAC sublayer also appends a PAD at the end of the MAC information field of sufficient length to ensure that the transmitted frame length satisfies a minimum frame size requirement (see 4.2.3.3). It also appends destination and source addresses, a length count field and a frame check sequence to provide for error detection. The frame is then handed to the Transmit Media Access Management component in the MAC sublayer for transmission.

Transmit Media Access Management then attempts to avoid contention with other traffic on the medium by monitoring the carrier sense signal provided by the PLS component and deferring to passing traffic. When the medium is clear, frame transmission is initiated (after a brief interframe delay to provide recovery time for other CSMA/CD MAC sublayers and for the physical medium). The MAC sublayer then provides a serial stream of bits to the PLS interface for transmission.

The PLS performs the task of actually generating the electrical signals on the medium which represent the bits of the frame. Simultaneously, it monitors the medium and generates the collison detect signal, which, in the contention-free case under discussion, remains off for the duration of the frame. A functional description of the Physical Layer is given in Sections 7, 8, and 9.

When transmission has completed without contention, the CSMA/CD MAC sublayer so informs the LLC sublayer using the LLC to MAC interface and awaits the next request for frame transmission.

4.1.2.1.2 Reception Without Contention.
At each receiving station, the arrival of a frame is first detected by the PLS, which responds by synchronizing with the incoming preamble, and by turning on the carrier sense signal. As the encoded bits arrive from the medium, they are decoded and translated back into binary data. The PLS passes subsequent bits up to the MAC sublayer, where the leading bits are discarded, up to and including the end of the preamble and Start Frame Delimiter.

Meanwhile, the Receive Media Access Management component of the MAC sublayer, having observed carrier sense, has been waiting for the incoming bits to be delivered. Receive Media Access Management collects bits from the PLS as long as the carrier sense signal remains on. When the carrier sense signal is removed, the frame is truncated to an octet boundary, if necessary, and passed to Receive Data Decapsulation for processing.

Receive Data Decapsulation checks the frame's Destination Address field to decide whether the frame should be received by this station. If so, it passes the

Destination Address (DA), the Source Address (SA), and the LLC data unit (LLCDU) to the LLC sublayer along with an appropriate status code indicating reception_complete or reception_too_long. It also checks for invalid MAC frames by inspecting the frame check sequence to detect any damage to the frame enroute, and by checking for proper octet-boundary alignment of the end of the frame. Frames with a valid FCS may also be checked for proper octet boundary alignment.

4.1.2.2 Access Interference and Recovery. If multiple stations attempt to transmit at the same time, it is possible for them to interfere with each others transmissions, in spite of their attempts to avoid this by deferring. When transmissions from two stations overlap, the resulting contention is called a collision. A given station can experience a collision during the initial part of its transmission (the collision window) before its transmitted signal has had time to propagate to all stations on the CSMA/CD medium. Once the collision window has passed, a transmitting station is said to have acquired the medium; subsequent collisions are avoided since all other (properly functioning) stations can be assumed to have noticed the signal (by way of carrier sense) and to be deferring to it. The time to acquire the medium is thus based on the round-trip propagation time of the physical layer whose elements include the PLS, PMA, and physical medium.

In the event of a collision, the transmitting station's Physical Layer initially notices the interference on the medium and then turns on the collision detect signal. This is noticed in turn by the Transmit Media Access Management component of the MAC sublayer, and collision handling begins. First, Transmit Media Access Management enforces the collision by transmitting a bit sequence called jam. In 4.4 an implementation that uses this enforcement procedure is provided. This ensures that the duration of the collision is sufficient to be noticed by the other transmitting station(s) involved in the collision. After the jam is sent, Transmit Media Access Management terminates the transmission and schedules another transmission attempt after a randomly selected time interval. Retransmission is attempted again in the face of repeated collisions. Since repeated collisions indicate a busy medium, however, Transmit Media Access Management attempts to adjust to the medium load by backing off (voluntarily delaying its own retransmissions to reduce its load on the medium). This is accomplished by expanding the interval from which the random retransmission time is selected on each successive transmit attempt. Eventually, either the transmission succeeds, or the attempt is abandoned on the assumption that the medium has failed or has become overloaded.

At the receiving end, the bits resulting from a collision are received and decoded by the PLS just as are the bits of a valid frame. Fragmentary frames received during collisions are distinguished from valid transmissions by the MAC sublayer's Receive Media Access Management component.

4.1.3 Relationships to LLC Sublayer and Physical Layer. The CSMA/CD MAC sublayer provides services to the LLC sublayer required for the transmission and reception of frames. Access to these services is specified in 4.3. The CSMA/CD MAC sublayer makes a best effort to acquire the medium and transfer a serial stream of bits to the PLS. Although certain errors are reported to the LLC, error recovery is not provided by MAC. Error recovery may be provided by the LLC or higher (sub) layers.

4.1.4. CSMA/CD Access Method Functional Capabilities. The following summary of the functional capabilities of the CSMA/CD MAC sublayer is intended as a quick reference guide to the capabilities of the standard:

(1) For frame transmission

(a) Accepts data from the LLC sublayer and constructs a frame

(b) Presents a bit-serial data stream to the physical layer for transmission on the medium

NOTE: Assumes data passed from the LLC sublayer are octet multiples.

(2) For frame reception

(a) Receives a bit-serial data stream from the physical layer

(b) Presents to the LLC sublayer frames that are either broadcast frames or directly addressed to the local station

(c) Discards or passes to Network Management all frames not addressed to the receiving station

(3) Defers transmission of a bit-serial stream whenever the physical medium is busy

(4) Appends proper FCS value to outgoing frames and verifies full octet boundary alignment.

(5) Checks incoming frames for transmission errors by way of FCS and verifies octet boundary alignment

(6) Delays transmission of frame bit stream for specified interframe gap period

(7) Halts transmission when collision is detected

(8) Schedules retransmission after a collision until a specified retry limit is reached

(9) Enforces collision to ensure propagation throughout network by sending jam message

(10) Discards received transmissions that are less than a minimum length

(11) Appends preamble, Start Frame Delimiter, DA, SA, length count, and FCS to all frames, and inserts pad field for frames whose LLC data length is less than a minimum value

(12) Removes preamble, Start Frame Delimiter, DA, SA, length count, FCS and pad field (if necessary) from received frames

4.2 CSMA/CD Media Access Control Method: Formal Specification

4.2.1 Introduction. A precise algorithmic definition is given in this section, providing procedural model for the CSMA/CD MAC process with a program in the computer language Pascal. See ANSI/IEEE Std 700X3.97-1983[2]. Note that whenever there is any apparent ambiguity concerning the definition of some aspect of the CSMA/CD MAC method, it is the Pascal procedural specification in 4.2.7 through 4.2.10 which should be consulted for the definitive statement. Sections 4.2.2 through 4.2.6 provide, in prose, a description of the access mechanism with the formal terminology to be used in the remaining subsections.

4.2.2 Overview of the Procedural Model. The functions of the CSMA/CD MAC method are presented below, modeled as a program written in the computer language Pascal. See ANSI/IEEE Std 770X3.97-1983[2]. This procedural model is intended as the primary specification of the functions to be provided in any CSMA/CD MAC sublayer implementation. It is important to distinguish, however, between the model and a real implementation. The model is optimized for simplicity and clarity of presentation, while any realistic implementation shall place heavier emphasis on such constraints as efficiency and suitability to a particular implementation technology or computer architecture. In this context, several important properties of the procedural model shall be considered.

4.2.2.1 Ground Rules for the Procedural Model

(1) First, it shall be emphasized that *the description of the MAC sublayer in a computer language is in no way intended to imply that procedures shall be implemented as a program executed by a computer.* The implementation may consist of any appropriate technology including hardware, firmware, software, or any combination.

(2) Similarly, it shall be emphasized that it is the behavior of any MAC sublayer implementations that shall match the standard, not their internal structure. The internal details of the procedural model are useful only to the extent that they help specify that behavior clearly and precisely.

(3) The handling of incoming and outgoing frames is rather stylized in the procedural model, in the sense that frames are handled as single entities by most of the MAC sublayer and are only serialized for presentation to the Physical Layer. In reality, many implementations will instead handle frames serially on a bit, octet, or word basis. This approach has not been reflected in the procedural model, since this only complicates the description of the functions without changing them in any way.

(4) The model consists of algorithms designed to be executed by a number of concurrent processes; these algorithms collectively implement the CSMA/CD procedure. The timing dependencies introduced by the need for concurrent activity are resolved in two ways

(a) *Processes Versus External Events.* It is assumed that the algorithms are executed "very fast" relative to external events, in the sense that a process never falls behind in its work and fails to respond to an external event in a timely manner. For example, when a frame is to be received, it is assumed that the Media Access procedure ReceiveFrame is always called well in advance before the frame in question has started to arrive.

(b) *Processes Versus Processes.* Among processes, no assumptions are made about relative speeds of execution. This means that each interaction between two processes shall be structured to work correctly independent of their respective speeds. Note, however, that the timing of interactions among processes is often, in part, an indirect reflection of the timing of external events, in which case appropriate timing assumptions may still be made.

It is intended that the concurrency in the model reflect the parallelism intrinsic to the task of implementing the LLC and MAC procedures, although the actual parallel structure of the implementations is likely to vary.

4.2.2.2 Use of Pascal in the Procedural Model. Several observations need to be made regarding the method with which Pascal is used for the model. Some of these observations are as follows:

(1) Some limitations of the language have been circumvented to simplify the specification:

(a) The elements of the program (variables and procedures, for example) are presented in logical groupings, in top-down order. Certain Pascal ordering restrictions have thus been circumvented to improve readability.

(b) The *process* and *cycle* constructs of the Pascal derivative Concurrent Pascal have been introduced to indicate the sites of autonomous concurrent activity. As used here, a process is simply a parameterless procedure that begins execution at "the beginning of time" rather than being invoked by a procedure call. A cycle statement represents the main body of a process and is executed repeatedly forever.

(c) The lack of variable array bounds in the language has been circumvented by treating frames as if they are always of a single fixed size (which is never actually specified). The size of a frame depends on the size of its data field, hence the value of the "pseudo-constant" frameSize should be thought of as varying in the long-term, even though it is fixed for any given frame.

(d) The use of a variant record to represent a frame (as fields and as bits) follows the spirit but not the letter of the Pascal Report, since it allows the underlying representation to be viewed as two different data types.

(2) The model makes no use of any explicit interprocess synchronization primitives. Instead, all interprocess interaction is done by way of carefully stylized manipulation of shared variables. For example, some variables are set by only one process and inspected by another process in such a manner that the net result is independent of their execution speeds. While such techniques are not generally suitable for the construction of large concurrent programs, they simplify the model and more nearly resemble the methods appropriate to the most likely implementation technologies (for example, microcode and hardware state-machines).

4.2.2.3 Organization of the Procedural Model. The procedural model used here is based on five cooperating concurrent processes. Three are actually defined in the MAC sublayer. The remaining two processes are provided by the clients of the MAC sublayer (which may include the LLC sublayer) and utilize the interface operations provided by the MAC sublayer. The five processes are thus:

(1) Frame Transmitter Process
(2) Frame Receiver Process
(3) Bit Transmitter Process
(4) Bit Receiver Process
(5) Deference Process

This organization of the model is illustrated in Fig 4-3 and reflects the fact that the communication of entire frames is initiated by the client of the MAC sublayer; while the timing of collision backoff and of individual bit transfers is based on interactions between the MAC sublayer and the Physical-Layer-dependent bit time.

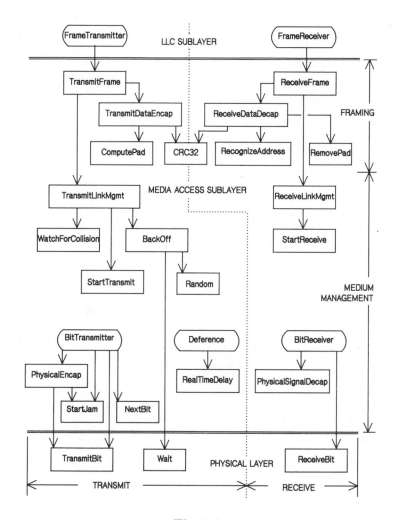

**Fig 4-3
Relationship Among CSMA/CD Procedures**

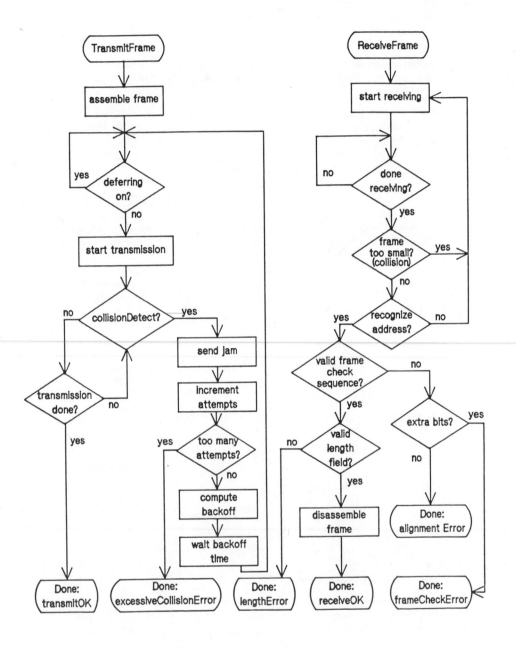

Fig 4-4
Control Flow Summary

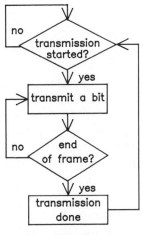

BitTransmitter process

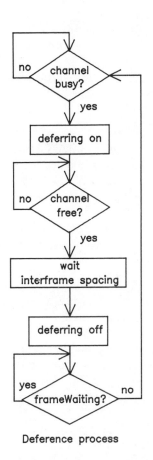

Deference process

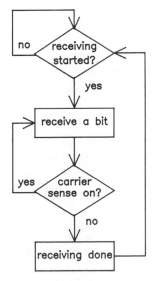

BitReceiver process

**Fig 4-5
Control Flow: MAC Sublayer**

Figure 4-3 depicts the static structure of the procedural model, showing how the various processes and procedures interact by invoking each other. Figures 4-4 and 4-5 summarize the dynamic behavior of the model during transmission and reception, focusing on the steps that shall be performed, rather than the procedural structure which performs them. The usage of the shared state variables is not depicted in the figures, but is described in the comments and prose in the following sections.

4.2.3 Frame Transmission Model. Frame transmission includes data encapsulation and Media Access management aspects.

(1) Transmit Data Encapsulation includes the assembly of the outgoing frame (from the values provided by the LLC sublayer) and frame check sequence generation.

(2) Transmit Media Access Management includes carrier deference, interframe spacing, collision detection and enforcement, and collision backoff and retransmission.

4.2.3.1 Transmit Data Encapsulation

4.2.3.1.1 Frame Assembly. The fields of the CSMA/CD MAC frame are set to the values provided by the LLC sublayer as arguments to the TransmitFrame operation (see 4.3), with the exception of the padding necessary to enforce the minimum frame size, and the frame check sequence, that is set to the CRC value generated by the MAC sublayer.

4.2.3.1.2 Frame Check Sequence Generation. The CRC value defined in 3.8 is generated and inserted in the frame check sequence field, following the fields supplied by the LLC sublayer.

4.2.3.2 Transmit Media Access Management

4.2.3.2.1 Carrier Deference. Even when it has nothing to transmit, the CSMA/CD MAC sublayer monitors the physical medium for traffic by watching the carrierSense signal provided by the PLS. Whenever the medium is busy, the CSMA/CD MAC sublayer defers to the passing frame by delaying any pending transmission of its own. After the last bit of the passing frame (that is, when carrierSense changes from true to false), the CSMA/CD MAC sublayer continues to defer for a proper interFrameSpacing, (see 4.2.3.2.2).

If, at the end of the interFrameSpacing, a frame is waiting to be transmitted, transmission is initiated independent of the value of carrierSense. When transmission has completed (or immediately, if there was nothing to transmit) the CSMA/CD MAC sublayer resumes its original monitoring of carrierSense.

When a frame is submitted by the LLC sublayer for transmission, the transmission is initiated as soon as possible, but in conformance with the rules of deference stated above.

NOTE: It is possible for the PLS carrier sense indication to fail to be asserted briefly during a collision on the media. If the Deference process simply times the interFrame gap based on this indication it is possible for a short interFrame gap to be generated, leading to a potential reception failure of a subsequent frame. To enhance system robustness the following optional measures, as specified in 4.2.8, are recommended when interFrame SpacingPart1 is other than zero.

(1) Upon completing a transmission, start timing the interpacket gap as soon as transmitting and carrierSense are both false.

(2) When timing an interFrame gap following reception, reset the inter-Frame gap timing if carrierSense becomes true during the first $2/3$ of the interFrame gap timing interval. During the final $1/3$ of the interval the timer shall not be reset to ensure fair access to the medium. An initial period shorter than $2/3$ of the interval is permissible including zero.

4.2.3.2.2. Interframe Spacing. As defined in 4.2.3.2.1, the rules for deferring to passing frames ensure a minimum interframe spacing of inter-FrameSpacing seconds. This is intended to provide interframe recovery time for other CSMA/CD sublayers and for the physical medium.

Note that interFrameSpacing is the minimum value of the interframe spacing. If necessary for implementation reasons, a transmitting sublayer may use a larger value with a resulting decrease in its throughput. The larger value is determined by the parameters of the implementation, see 4.4.

4.2.3.2.3. Collision Handling. Once a CSMA/CD sublayer has finished deferring and has started transmission, it is still possible for it to experience contention for the medium. Collisions can occur until acquisition of the network has been accomplished through the deference of all other stations' CSMA/CD sublayers.

The dynamics of collision handling are largely determined by a single parameter called the slot time. This single parameter describes three important aspects of collision handling

(1) It is an upper bound on the acquisition time of the medium

(2) It is an upper bound on the length of a frame fragment generated by a collision

(3) It is the scheduling quantum for retransmission.

To fulfill all three functions, the slot time shall be larger than the sum of the Physical Layer round-trip propagation time and the Media Access sublayer maximum jam time. The slot time is determined by the parameters of the implementation, see 4.4.

4.2.3.2.4 Collision Detection and Enforcement. Collisions are detected by monitoring the collisionDetect signal provided by the Physical Layer. When a collision is detected during a frame transmission, the transmission is not terminated immediately. Instead, the transmission continues until additional bits specified by jamSize have been transmitted (counting from the time collisionDetect went on). This collision enforcement or jam guarantees that the duration of the collision is sufficient to ensure its detection by all transmitting stations on the network. The content of the jam is unspecified; it may be any fixed or variable pattern convenient to the Media Access implementation, however, the implementation shall not be intentionally designed to be the 32-bit CRC value corresponding to the (partial) frame transmitted prior to the jam.

4.2.3.2.5 Collision Backoff and Retransmission. When a transmission attempt has terminated due to a collision, it is retried by the transmitting CSMA/CD MAC sublayer until either it is successful or a maximum number of attempts (attemptLimit) have been made and all have terminated due to collisions. Note that all attempts to transmit a given frame are completed before any subsequent outgoing frames are transmitted. The scheduling of the retransmissions is determined by a controlled randomization process called "truncated binary exponential backoff." At the end of enforcing a collision (jamming), the CSMA/CD MAC sublayer delays before attempting to retransmit the frame. The delay is an integer multiple of slotTime. The number of slot times to delay before the nth retransmission attempt is chosen as a uniformly distributed random integer r in the range

$$0 \leq r < 2^k$$

where

$k = \min (n, 10)$

If all attemptLimit attempts fail, this event is reported as an error. Algorithms used to generate the integer r should be designed to minimize the correlation between the numbers generated by any two stations at any given time.

Note that the values given above define the most aggressive behavior that a station may exhibit in attempting to retransmit after a collision. In the course of implementing the retransmission scheduling procedure, a station may introduce extra delays which will degrade its own throughput, but in no case may a station's retransmission scheduling result in a lower average delay between retransmission attempts than the procedure defined above.

4.2.3.3 Minimum Frame Size. The CSMA/CD Media Access mechanism requires that a minimum frame length of minFrameSize bits be transmitted. If frameSize is less than minFrameSize, then the CSMA/CD MAC sublayer shall append extra bits in units of octets, after the end of the LLC data field but prior to calculating, and appending, the FCS. The number of extra bits shall be sufficient to ensure that the frame, from the DA field through the FCS field inclusive, is at least minFrameSize bits. The content of the pad is unspecified.

4.2.4 Frame Reception Model. CSMA/CD MAC sublayer frame reception includes both data decapsulation and Media Access management aspects:

(1) Receive Data Decapsulation comprises address recognition, frame check sequence validation, and frame disassembly to pass the fields of the received frame to the LLC sublayer.

(2) Receive Media Access Management comprises recognition of collision fragments from incoming frames and truncation of frames to octet boundaries.

4.2.4.1 Receive Data Decapsulation

4.2.4.1.1 Address Recognition. The CSMA/CD MAC sublayer is capable of recognizing individual and group addresses.

(1) *Individual Addresses.* The CSMA/CD MAC sublayer recognizes and accepts any frame whose DA field contains the individual address of the station.

(2) *Group Addresses.* The CSMA/CD MAC sublayer recognizes and accepts any frame whose DA field contains the Broadcast address.

The CSMA/CD MAC sublayer is capable of activating some number of group addresses as specified by higher layers. The CSMA/CD MAC sublayer recognizes and accepts any frame whose DA field contains an active group address. An active group address may be deactivated.

4.2.4.1.2 Frame Check Sequence Validation. FCS validation is essentially identical to FCS generation. If the bits of the incoming frame (exclusive of the FCS field itself) do not generate a CRC value identical to the one received, an error has occurred and the frame is identified as invalid.

4.2.4.1.3 Frame Disassembly. Upon recognition of the Start Frame Delimiter at the end of the preamble sequence, the CSMA/CD MAC sublayer accepts the frame. If there are no errors, the frame is disassembled and the fields are passed to the LLC sublayer by way of the output parameters of the ReceiveFrame operation.

4.2.4.2 Receive Media Access Management

4.2.4.2.1 Framing. The CSMA/CD sublayer recognizes the boundaries of an incoming frame by monitoring the carrierSense signal provided by the PLS. There are two possible length errors that can occur, that indicate ill-framed data: the frame may be too long, or its length may not be an integer number of octets.

(1) *Maximum Frame Size.* The receiving CSMA/CD sublayer is not required to enforce the frame size limit, but it is allowed to truncate frames longer than maxFrameSize octets and report this event as an (implementation-dependent) error.

(2) *Integer Number of Octets in Frame.* Since the format of a valid frame specifies an integer number of octets, only a collision or an error can produce a frame with a length that is not an integer multiple of 8 bits. Complete frames (that is, not rejected as collision fragments; see 4.2.4.2.2) that do not contain an integer number of octets are truncated to the nearest octet boundary. If frame check sequence validation detects an error in such a frame, the status code alignmentError is reported.

4.2.4.2.2 Collision Filtering. The smallest valid frame shall be at least one slotTime in length. This determines the minFrameSize. Any frame containing less than minFrameSize bits is presumed to be a fragment resulting from a collision. Since occasional collisions are a normal part of the Media Access management procedure, the discarding of such a fragment is not reported as an error to the LLC sublayer.

4.2.5 Preamble Generation. In a LAN implementation, most of the Physical Layer components are allowed to provide valid output some number of bit times after being presented valid input signals. Thus it is necessary for a preamble to be sent before the start of data, to allow the PLS circuitry to reach its steady-state. Upon request by TransmitLinkMgmt to transmit the first bit of a new frame, PhysicalSignalEncap shall first transmit the preamble, a bit sequence used for physical medium stabilization and synchronization, followed by the start frame delimiter. If, while transmitting the preamble, the PLS asserts the collision detect signal, any remaining preamble bits shall be sent. The preamble pattern is:

10101010 10101010 10101010 10101010 10101010 10101010 10101010

The bits are transmitted in order, from left to right. The nature of the pattern is such that, for Manchester encoding, it appears as a periodic waveform on the medium that enables bit synchronization. It should be noted that the preamble ends with a "0".

4.2.6 Start Frame Sequence. The PLS recognizes the presence of activity on the medium through the carrier sense signal. This is the first indication that the frame reception process should begin. Upon reception of the sequence 10101011 immediately following a latter part of the preamble pattern, PhysicalSignalDecap shall begin passing successive bits to ReceiveLinkMgmt for passing to the LLC sublayer.

4.2.7 Global Declarations. This section provides detailed formal specifications for the CSMA/CD MAC sublayer. It is a specification of generic features and parameters to be used in systems implementing this media access method. Section 4.4 provides values for these sets of parameters for recommended implementations of this media access mechanism.

4.2.7.1 Common Constants and Types. The following declarations of constants and types are used by the frame transmission and reception sections of each CSMA/CD sublayer:

const
      addressSize = ... ; {16 or 48 bits in compliance with 4.3.3}
      lengthSize = 16; {in bits}
      LLCdataSize = ...; {LLC Data, see 4.2.2.2, (1)(c)}
      padSize = ...; {in bits, = max (0, minFrameSize – (2·addressSize
                     + lengthSize + LLCdataSize + crcSize))}
      dataSize = ...; {=LLCdataSize + padSize}
      crcSize = 32; {32 bit CRC = 4 octets}
      frameSize = ...; {= 2·addressSize + lengthSize + dataSize + crcSize,
                  see 4.2.2.2(1)}
      minFrameSize = ... ; {in bits, implementation dependent, see 4.4}
      slotTime = ... ; {unit of time for collision handling, implementation
                  dependent, see Section 4.4}

preambleSize = ... ; {in bits, physical medium dependent}
sfdSize = 8; {8 bit start frame delimiter}
headerSize = ...; {sum of preambleSize and sfdSize}

type
    Bit = 0..1;
    AddressValue = *array* [1..addressSize] *of* Bit;
    LengthValue = *array* [1..lengthSize] *of* Bit;
    DataValue = *array* [1..dataSize] *of* Bit;
    CRCValue = *array* [1..crcSize] *of* Bit;
    PreambleValue = *array* [1..preambleSize] *of* Bit;
    SfdValue = *array* [1..sfdSize] *of* Bit;
    ViewPoint = (fields, bits); {Two ways to view the contents of a frame}
    HeaderViewPoint = (headerFields, headerBits);
    Frame = *record* {Format of Media Access frame}
      case view: ViewPoint *of*
        fields: (
          destinationField: AddressValue;
          sourceField: AddressValue;
          lengthField: LengthValue;
          dataField: DataValue;
          fcsField: CRCValue);
        bits: (contents: *array* [1..frameSize] *of* Bit)
      end; {Frame}
    Header = *record* {Format of preamble and start frame delimiter}
      case headerView : HeaderViewPoint *of*
      headerFields : (
        preamble : PreambleValue;
        sfd : SfdValue);
      headerBits : (
        headerContents : *array* [1..headerSize] *of* Bit)
      end; {defines header for MAC frame}

4.2.7.2 Transmit State Variables. The following items are specific to frame transmission. (See also 4.4.)

const
    interFrameSpacing = ... ; {minimum time between frames}
    interFrameSpacingPart1 =...;{duration of first portion of interFrame
                   timing. In range 0 up to 2/3
                   interFrameSpacing}
    interFrameSpacingPart2 =...;{duration of remainder of interFrame
                   timing. Equal to interFrameSpacing
                   - interFrameSpacingPart1}
    attemptLimit = ... ; {Max number of times to attempt transmission}

backOffLimit = ... ; {Limit on number of times to back off}
jamSize = ... ; {in bits: the value depends upon medium and collision
               detect implementation}

var
outgoingFrame: Frame; {The frame to be transmitted}
outgoingHeader: Header;
currentTransmitBit, lastTransmitBit: 1..frameSize;
{Positions of current and last outgoing bits in outgoingFrame}
lastHeaderBit: 1..headerSize;
deferring: Boolean; {Implies any pending transmission must wait for the
               medium to clear}
frameWaiting: Boolean; {Indicates that outgoingFrame is deferring}
attempts: 0..attemptLimit; {Number of transmission attempts on
               outgoingFrame}
newCollision: Boolean; {Indicates that a collision has occured but has
               not yet been jammed}
transmitSucceeding: Boolean; {Running indicator of whether
               transmission is succeeding}

4.2.7.3 Receive State Variables. The following items are specific to
frame reception. (See also 4.4.)

var
incomingFrame: Frame; {The frame being received}
currentReceiveBit: 1..frameSize; {Position of current bit in
               incomingFrame}
receiving: Boolean; {Indicates that a frame reception is in progress}
excessBits: 0..7; {Count of excess trailing bits beyond octet boundary}
receiveSucceeding: Boolean; {Running indicator of whether reception is
               succeeding}
validLength: Boolean; {Indicator of whether received frame has a length
               error}

4.2.7.4 Summary of Interlayer Interfaces.
(1) The interface to the LLC sublayer, defined in 4.3.2, is summarized below:

type
TransmitStatus = (transmitOK, excessiveCollisionError);
               {Result of TransmitFrame operation}
ReceiveStatus = (receiveOK, lengthError, frameCheckError,
               alignmentError);
               {Result of ReceiveFrame operation}

function TransmitFrame (
destinationParam: AddressValue;
sourceParam: AddressValue;
lengthParam: LengthValue;
dataParam: DataValue): TransmitStatus; {Transmits one frame}

function ReceiveFrame (
  var destinationParam: AddressValue;
  var sourceParam: AddressValue;
  var lengthParam: LengthValue;
  var dataParam: DataValue): ReceiveStatus; {Receives one frame}

(2) The interface to the Physical Layer, defined in 4.3.3, is summarized below.

var
  carrierSense: Boolean; {Indicates incoming bits}
  transmitting: Boolean; {Indicates outgoing bits}
  wasTransmitting: Boolean; {Indicates transmission in progress or just
                            completed}
  collisionDetect: Boolean; {Indicates medium contention}
  procedure TransmitBit (bitParam: Bit); {Transmits one bit}
  function ReceiveBit: Bit; {Receives one bit}
  procedure Wait (bitTimes: integer); {Waits for indicated number of
                            bit-times}

4.2.7.5 State Variable Initialization. The procedure Initialize must be run when the MAC sublayer begins operation, before any of the processes begin execution. Initialize sets certain crucial shared state variables to their initial values. (All other global variables are appropriately reinitialized before each use.) Initialize then waits for the the medium to be idle, and starts operation of the various processes.

procedure Initialize;
begin
  frameWaiting := false;
  deferring := false;
  newCollision := false;
  transmitting := false; {In interface to Physical Layer; see below}
  receiving := false;
  while carrierSense *do* nothing;
  {Start execution of all processes}
end; {Initialize}

4.2.8 Frame Transmission. The algorithms in this section define MAC sublayer frame transmission. The function TransmitFrame implements the frame transmission operation provided to the LLC sublayer:

function TransmitFrame (
  destinationParam: AddressValue;
  sourceParam: AddressValue;
  lengthParam: LengthValue;
  dataParam: DataValue): TransmitStatus;
  procedure TransmitDataEncap; ... {nested procedure; see body below}
begin

```
    TransmitDataEncap;
    TransmitFrame := TransmitLinkMgmt
  end; {TransmitFrame}
```

First, TransmitFrame calls the internal procedure TransmitDataEncap to construct the frame. Next, TransmitLinkMgmt is called to perform the actual transmission. The TransmitStatus returned indicates the success or failure of the transmission attempt.

TransmitDataEncap builds the frame and places the 32-bit CRC in the frame check sequence field:

```
procedure TransmitDataEncap;
begin
  with outgoingFrame do
  begin {assemble frame}
    view := fields;
    destinationField := destinationParam;
    sourceField := sourceParam;
    lengthField: = lengthParam;
    dataField := ComputePad (lengthParam, dataParam);
    fcsField := CRC32(outgoingFrame);
    view := bits
  end {assemble frame}
  with outgoingHeader do
  begin
    headerView: = headerFields;
    preamble: = ...; {* '1010...10', LSB to MSB*}
    sfd: = ...; {* '10101011', LSB to MSB*}
    headerView: = headerBits
  end
end; {TransmitDataEncap}
```

ComputePad appends an array of arbitrary bits to the LLCdataField to pad the frame to the minimum frame size.

```
function ComputePad(
    var lengthParam:LengthValue
    var dataParam:DataValue) :DataValue;
begin
    ComputePad: = {Append an array of size padSize of arbitrary bits to the
                  LLCdataField}
  end;{ComputePadParam}
```

TransmitLinkMgmt attempts to transmit the frame, deferring first to any passing traffic. If a collision occurs, transmission is terminated properly and retransmission is scheduled following a suitable backoff interval:

```
function TransmitLinkMgmt: TransmitStatus;
```

```
begin
  attempts := 0; transmitSucceeding := false;
  while(attemptsattemptLimit) and (not transmitSucceeding)do
  begin {loop}
    if attempts > 0 then BackOff;
    frameWaiting := true;
    while deferring do nothing;{defer to passing frame, if any}
    frameWaiting := false;
    StartTransmit;
    while transmitting do WatchForCollision;
    attempts := attempts+1
  end; {loop}
  if transmitSucceeding then TransmitLinkMgmt := transmitOK
  else TransmitLinkMgmt := excessiveCollisionError
end; {TransmitLinkMgmt}
```

Each time a frame transmission attempt is initiated, StartTransmit is called to alert the BitTransmitter process that bit transmission should begin:

```
procedure StartTransmit;
begin
  currentTransmitBit := 1;
  lastTransmitBit := frameSize;
  transmitSucceeding := true;
  transmitting := true;
  lastHeaderBit: = headerSize
end; {StartTransmit}
```

Once frame transmission has been initiated, TransmitLinkMgmt monitors the medium for contention by repeatedly calling WatchForCollision:

```
procedure WatchForCollision;
begin
  if transmitSucceeding and collisionDetect then
  begin
    newCollision := true;
    transmitSucceeding := false
  end
end; {WatchForCollision}
```

WatchForCollision, upon detecting a collision, updates newCollision to insure proper jamming by the BitTransmitter process.

After transmission of the jam has been completed, if TransmitLinkMgmt determines that another attempt should be made, BackOff is called to schedule the next attempt to retransmit the frame.

var maxBackOff: 2..1024; {Working variable of BackOff}

47

```
procedure BackOff;
begin
 if attempts = 1 then maxBackOff := 2
 else if attempts ≤ backOffLimit
 then maxBackOff := maxBackOff × 2;
 Wait(slotTime × Random(0, maxBackOff))
end; {BackOff}

function Random (low, high: integer): integer;

begin
   Random := ...{uniformly distributed random integer r such that
               low ≤ r < high}
end; {Random}
```

BackOff performs the truncated binary exponential backoff computation and then waits for the selected multiple of the slot time.

The Deference process runs asynchronously to continuously compute the proper value for the variable deferring.

```
process Deference;
 begin
   cycle{main loop}
       while not carrierSense do nothing; {watch for carrier to appear}
       deferring := true; {delay start of new transmissions}
       wasTransmitting:=transmitting;
       while carrierSense or transmitting do
           wasTransmitting: = wasTransmitting or transmitting;
       if wasTransmitting do
           begin
               StartRealTimeDelay; {time out first part interframe gap}
               while RealTimeDelay(interFrameSpacingPart1) do nothing
           end
       else
           begin
               StartRealTimeDelay;
               repeat
                  while carrierSense do StartRealTimeDelay
               until not RealTimeDelay(interFrameSpacingPart1)
           end;
       StartRealTimeDelay; {time out second part interframe gap}
       while RealTimeDelay(interFrameSpacingPart2) do nothing;
       deferring: = false; {allow new transmissions to proceed}
       while frameWaiting do nothing; {allow waiting transmission if any}
   end {main loop}
 end; {Deference}
```

procedure StartRealTimeDelay
  begin
    {reset the realtimetimer and start it timing}
  end; {StartRealTimeDelay}

function RealTimeDelay (μsec:real): Boolean;
  begin
    {return the value true if the specified number of microseconds have not
    elapsed since the most recent invocation of StartRealTimeDelay,
    otherwise return the value false}
  end; {RealTimeDelay}

The BitTransmitter process runs asynchronously, transmitting bits at a rate
determined by the Physical Layer's TransmitBit operation:

process BitTransmitter;
begin
  cycle {outer loop}
    If transmitting *then*
    begin {inner loop}
      PhysicalSignalEncap; {Send preamble and start of frame delimiter}
      while transmitting *do*
      begin
        TransmitBit(outgoingFrame[currentTransmitBit]);
                  {send next bit to Physical Layer}
        if newCollision *then* StartJam *else* NextBit
      end;
    end; {inner loop}
  end; {outer loop}
end; {BitTransmitter}

procedure PhysicalSignalEncap;
begin
  while currentTransmitBit $\leq$ lastHeaderBit *do*
  begin
    TransmitBit(outgoingHeader[currentTransmitBit]);
             {transmit header one bit at a time}
    currentTransmitBit := currentTransmitBit + 1;
  end
  if newCollision *then* StartJam *else*
  currentTransmitBit := 1
end; {PhysicalSignalEncap}

procedure NextBit;
begin
  currentTransmitBit := currentTransmitBit+1;
  transmitting := (currentTransmitBit $\leq$ lastTransmitBit)
end; {NextBit}

```
procedure StartJam;
begin
  currentTransmitBit := 1;
  lastTransmitBit := jamSize;
  newCollision := false
end; {StartJam}
```

BitTransmitter, upon detecting a new collision, immediately enforces it by calling StartJam to initiate the transmission of the jam. The jam should contain a sufficient number of bits of arbitrary data so that it is assured that both communicating stations detect the collision (StartJam uses the first set of bits of the frame up to jamSize, merely to simplify this program).

4.2.9 Frame Reception. The algorithms in this section define CSMA/CD Media Access sublayer frame reception.

The procedure ReceiveFrame implements the frame reception operation provided to the LLC sublayer:

```
function ReceiveFrame (
    var destinationParam: AddressValue;
    var sourceParam: AddressValue;
    var lengthParam: LengthValue;
    var dataParam: DataValue): ReceiveStatus;
  function ReceiveDataDecap: ReceiveStatus; ... {nested function;
                                            see body below}
begin
 repeat
    ReceiveLinkMgmt;
    ReceiveFrame := ReceiveDataDecap;
  until receiveSucceeding
end; {ReceiveFrame}
```

ReceiveFrame calls ReceiveLinkMgmt to receive the next valid frame, and then calls the internal procedure ReceiveDataDecap to return the frame's fields to the LLC sublayer if the frame's address indicates that it should do so. The returned ReceiveStatus indicates the presence or absence of detected transmission errors in the frame.

```
function ReceiveDataDecap: ReceiveStatus;
begin
  receiveSucceeding := RecognizeAddress (incomingFrame,
                                    destinationField);
   if receiveSucceeding then with incomingFrame do
   begin {disassemble frame}
    view :=fields;
    destinationParam := destinationField;
    sourceParam := sourceField;
```

```
    lengthParam: = lengthField;
    dataParam := RemovePad (lengthField, dataField);
    if fcsField = CRC32(incomingFrame) then
    begin
        if validLength then ReceiveDataDecap: = receiveOK
        else ReceiveDataDecap: = lengthError
    end
    else
    begin
        if excessBits = 0 then ReceiveDataDecap :=
        frameCheckError
        else ReceiveDataDecap := alignmentError;
    end;
    view: = bits
  end {disassemble frame}
end; {ReceiveDataDecap}

function RecognizeAddress (address: AddressValue): Boolean;
begin
    RecognizeAddress := ... {Returns true for the set of physical, broadcast,
                            and multicast-group addresses corresponding
                            to this station}
end;{RecognizeAddress}

function RemovePad(
        var lengthParam:LengthValue
        var dataParam:DataValue):DataValue;
begin
        validLength:={Check to determine if value represented by
                        lengthParam matches received LLCdataSize};
        if validLength then
                RemovePad:={truncate the dataParam (when present) to value
                            represented by lengthParam (in octets) and
                            return the result}
                else
                RemovePad:=dataParam
    end; {RemovePad}
```

ReceiveLinkMgmt attempts repeatedly to receive the bits of a frame,
discarding any fragments from collisions by comparing them to the minimum
valid frame size:

```
procedure ReceiveLinkMgmt;
begin
 repeat
    StartReceive;
    while receiving do nothing; {wait for frame to finish arriving}
```

```
        excessBits := frameSize mod 8;
        frameSize :=frameSize - excessBits;{truncate to octet boundary}
        receiveSucceeding := (frameSize ≥ minFrameSize);
                            {reject collision fragments}
    until receiveSucceeding
    end; {ReceiveLinkMgmt}

    procedure StartReceive;
    begin
     currentReceiveBit := 1;
     receiving := true
    end; {StartReceive}
```

The BitReceiver process runs asynchronously, receiving bits from the medium at the rate determined by the Physical Layer's ReceiveBit operation:

```
    process BitReceiver;
     var b: Bit;
    begin
     cycle {outer loop}
       while receiving do
       begin {inner loop}
       If currentReceiveBit = 1 then
         PhysicalSignalDecap; {Strip off the preamble and start frame
                             delimiter}
          b := ReceiveBit; {Get next bit from physical Media Access}
          if carrierSense then
          begin{append bit to frame}
           incomingFrame[currentReceiveBit] := b;
           currentReceiveBit := currentReceiveBit+1
          end; {append bit to frame}
          receiving := carrierSense
       end {inner loop}
       frameSize: = currentReceiveBit -1
     end {outer loop}
    end; {BitReceiver}

    Procedure PhysicalSignalDecap;
    begin
     {Receive one bit at a time from physical medium until a valid sfd is
       detected, discard bits and return}
    end; {PhysicalSignalDecap}
```

4.2.10 Common Procedures. The function CRC32 is used by both the transmit and receive algorithms to generate a 32 bit CRC value:

```
    function CRC32 (f: Frame): CRCValue;
    begin
     CRC32 := {The 32-bit CRC}
    end; {CRC32}
```

Purely to enhance readability, the following procedure is also defined:

procedure nothing; *begin end*;

The idle state of a process (that is, while waiting for some event) is cast as repeated calls on this procedure.

4.3 Interfaces to/from Adjacent Layers

4.3.1 Overview. The purpose of this section is to provide precise definitions of the interfaces between the architectural layers defined in Section 1 in compliance with the Media Access Service Specification given in Section 2. In addition, the services required from the physical medium are defined.

The notation used here is the Pascal language (see ANSI/IEEE Std 770X3.97-1983[2]), in keeping with the procedural nature of the formal and MAC sublayers specification (see 4.2). Each interface is described as a set of procedures or shared variables, or both, that collectively provide the only valid interactions between layers. The accompanying text describes the meaning of each procedure or variable and points out any implicit interactions among them.

Note that the description of the interfaces in Pascal is a notational technique, and in no way implies that they can or should be implemented in software. This point is discussed more fully in 4.2, that provides complete Pascal declarations for the data types used in the remainder of this section. Note also that the "synchronous" (one frame at a time) nature of the frame transmission and reception operations is a property of the architectural interface between the LLC and MAC sublayers, and need not be reflected in the implementation interface between a station and its sublayer.

4.3.2 Services Provided by the MAC Sublayer. The services provided to the LLC sublayer by the MAC sublayer are transmission and reception of LLC frames. The interface through which the LLC sublayer uses the facilities of the MAC sublayer therefore consists of a pair of functions.

Functions:
  TransmitFrame
  ReceiveFrame

Each of these functions has the components of a LLC frame as its parameters (input or output), and returns a status code as its result. Note that the service_class defined in 2.3.1 is ignored by CSMA/CD MAC.

The LLC sublayer transmits a frame by invoking TransmitFrame:

function TransmitFrame (
  destinationParam: AddressValue;
  sourceParam: AddressValue;
  lengthParam: LengthValue;
  dataParam: DataValue): TransmitStatus;

The TransmitFrame operation is synchronous. Its duration is the entire attempt to transmit the frame; when the operation completes, transmission has either succeeded or failed, as indicated by the resulting status code:

type TransmitStatus = (transmitOK, excessiveCollisionError);

Successful transmission is indicated by the status code transmitOK; the code excessiveCollisionError indicates that the transmission attempt was aborted due to excessive collisions, because of heavy traffic or a network failure.

The LLC sublayer accepts incoming frames by invoking ReceiveFrame:

function ReceiveFrame (
 var destinationParam: AddressValue;
 var sourceParam: AddressValue;
 var length Param: LengthValue;
 var dataParam): DataValue): ReceiveStatus;

The ReceiveFrame operation is synchronous. The operation does not complete until a frame has been received. The fields of the frame are delivered by way of the output parameters with a status code:

type ReceiveStatus = (receiveOK, lengthError, frameCheckError,
     alignmentError);

Successful reception is indicated by the status code receiveOK. The code frameCheckError indicates that the frame received was damaged by a transmission error. The code alignmentError indicates that the frame received was damaged, and that in addition, its length was not an integer number of octets. The lengthError indicates the lengthParam value was inconsistent with the frameSize of the received frame.

4.3.3 Services Required from the Physical Layer. The interface through which the CSMA/CD MAC sublayer uses the facilities of the Physical Layer consists of a function, a pair of procedures, and three Boolean variables.

Function:	*Procedures:*	*Variables:*
ReceiveBit	TransmitBit	collisionDetect
	Wait	carrierSense
		transmitting

During transmission, the contents of an outgoing frame are passed from the MAC sublayer to the Physical Layer by way of repeated use of the TransmitBit operation:

procedure TransmitBit (bitParam: Bit);

Each invocation of TransmitBit passes one new bit of the outgoing frame to the Physical Layer. The TransmitBit operation is synchronous. The duration of the operation is the entire transmission of the bit. The operation completes, when the Physical Layer is ready to accept the next bit and it transfers control to the MAC sublayer.

The overall event of data being transmitted is signaled to the Physical Layer by way of the variable transmitting:

var transmitting: Boolean;

Before sending the first bit of a frame, the MAC sublayer sets transmitting to true, to inform the Physical Media Access that a stream of bits will be presented by way of the TransmitBit operation. After the last bit of the frame has been presented, the MAC sublayer sets transmitting to false to indicate the end of the frame.

The presence of a collision in the physical medium is signaled to the MAC sublayer by the variable collisionDetect:

var collisionDetect: Boolean;

The collisionDetect signal remains true during the duration of the collision.

NOTE: Since an entire collision may occur during preamble generation, the MAC sublayer shall handle this possibility by monitoring collisionDetect concurrently with its transmission of outgoing bits. See 4.2 for details.

The collisionDetect signal is generated only during transmission and is never true at any other time; in particular, it cannot be used during frame reception to detect collisions between overlapping transmissions from two or more other stations.

During reception, the contents of an incoming frame are retrieved from the Physical Layer by the MAC sublayer by way of repeated use of the ReceiveBit operation:

function ReceiveBit: Bit;

Each invocation of ReceiveBit retrieves one new bit of the incoming frame from the Physical Layer. The ReceiveBit operation is synchronous. Its duration is the entire reception of a single bit. Upon receiving a bit, the MAC sublayer shall immediately request the next bit until all bits of the frame have been received. (See 4.2 for details.)

The overall event of data being received is signaled to the MAC sublayer by the variable carrierSense:

var carrierSense: Boolean;

When the Physical Layer sets carrierSense to true, the MAC sublayer shall immediately begin retrieving the incoming bits by the ReceiveBit operation. When carrierSense subsequently becomes false, the MAC sublayer can begin processing the received bits as a completed frame. Note that the true/false transitions of carrierSense are not defined to be precisely synchronized with the beginning and end of the frame, but may precede the beginning and lag the end, respectively. If an invocation of ReceiveBit is pending when carrierSense becomes false, ReceiveBit returns an undefined value, which should be discarded by the MAC sublayer. (See 4.2 for details.)

The MAC sublayer shall also monitor the value of carrierSense to defer its own transmissions when the medium is busy.

The Physical Layer also provides the procedure Wait:

procedure Wait (bitTimes: integer);

This procedure waits for the specified number of bit times. This allows the MAC sublayer to measure time intervals in units of the (physical-medium-dependent) bit time.

Another important property of the Physical Layer which is an implicit part of the interface presented to the MAC sublayer is the round-trip propagation time of the physical medium. Its value represents the maximum time required for a signal to propagate from one end of the network to the other, and for a collision to propagate back. The round-trip propagation time is primarily (but not entirely) a function of the physical size of the network. The round-trip propagation time of the Physical Layer is defined in 4.4 for a selection of physical media.

4.4 Specific Implementations

4.4.1 Compatibility Overview. To provide total compatibility at all levels of the standard, it is required that each network component implementing the CSMA/CD MAC sublayer procedure adheres rigidly to these specifications. The information in 4.4.2.1 provides design parameters for a specific implementation of this access method. Variations from these values result in a system implementation that violates the standard.

4.4.2 Allowable Implementations

4.4.2.1 Parameterized Values. The following table identifies the parameter values that shall be used in the 10 Mb/s implementation (type 10BASE5) of a CSMA/CD MAC procedure. The primary assumptions are that the physical medium is a baseband coaxial cable with properties given in the Physical Layer section(s) of this standard.

Parameters	Values
slotTime	512 bit times
interFrameGap	9.6 μs
attemptLimit	16
backoffLimit	10
jamSize	32 bits
maxFrameSize	1518 octets
minFrameSize	512 bits (64 octets)
addressSize	48 bits

> **WARNING:** Any deviation from the above values specified for a 10 Mb/s system may affect proper operation of the LAN.

4.4.2.2 Parameterized Values. Other Implementations (under consideration).

5. Network Management

In CSMA/CD, no peer management functions[9] are necessary for initiating, terminating, or handling abnormal conditions. Monitoring of ongoing activities is done by the carrier sense and collision detect mechanisms. These are necessary for the normal operation of the protocol. Hence they are not considered as part of network management. Also, other monitoring of ongoing activities, which are media independent, should be done by LLC or higher layers. This allows the media access method to be implemented in a cost effective manner.

It is useful to identify local or nodal management activities for the LAN. Protocols and interfaces to support such functions have not yet been defined. Defining local or nodal management functions are very useful for designers and users, although such protocols are not necessary for compatibility between two systems.

Standardizing these functions will promote compatibility of components (for example, LSI controller chips) which implement portions of this standard. It will also make practical high level protocols for distributed control and maintenance of LANs.

6. PLS Service Specifications

6.1 Scope and Field of Application. This section specifies the services provided by the Physical Signaling (PLS) sublayer to the MAC sublayer for the CSMA/CD section of the Local Area Network Standard, Fig 6-1. The services are described in an abstract way and do not imply any particular implementation.

6.2. Overview of the Service

6.2.1 General Description of Services Provided by the Layer. The services provided by the PLS sublayer allow the local MAC sublayer entity to exchange data bits (PLS data_units) with peer MAC sublayer entities.

6.2.2 Model Used for the Service Specification. The model used in this service specification is identical to that used in 1.2.

6.2.3 Overview of Interactions. The primitives associated with the MAC sublayer to PLS sublayer interface fall into two basic categories:

(1) Service primitives that support MAC peer-to-peer interactions

(2) Service primitives that have local significance and support sublayer-to-sublayer interactions

---

[9] The elaboration of management functions is under active consideration by the CSMA/CD standards committee.

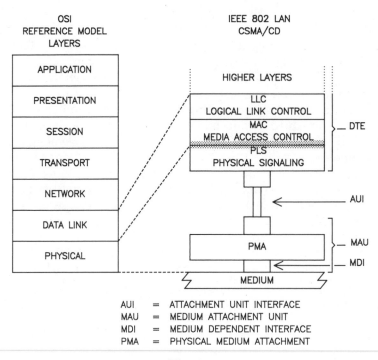

AUI = ATTACHMENT UNIT INTERFACE
MAU = MEDIUM ATTACHMENT UNIT
MDI = MEDIUM DEPENDENT INTERFACE
PMA = PHYSICAL MEDIUM ATTACHMENT

Fig 6-1
Service Specification Relationship to the LAN Model

The following primitives are grouped into these two categories:
(1) Peer-to-Peer

PLS_DATA.request
PLS_DATA.confirm
PLS_DATA.indication

(2) Sublayer-to-Sublayer

PLS_CARRIER.indication
PLS_SIGNAL.indication

The PLS_DATA primitives support the transfer of data from a single MAC sublayer entity to all other peer MAC sublayer entities contained within the same local area network defined by the broadcast medium.

NOTE: This also means that all bits transfered from a given MAC sublayer entity will in turn be received by the entity itself.

The PLS_CARRIER and the PLS_SIGNAL primitives provide information needed by the local MAC sublayer entity to perform the media access functions.

6.2.4 Basic Services and Options. All of the service primitives described in this section are considered mandatory.

6.3 Detailed Service Specification

6.3.1 Peer-To-Peer Service Primitives

6.3.1.1 PLS_DATA.request

6.3.1.1.1 Function. This primitive defines the transfer of data from the MAC sublayer to the local PLS entity.

6.3.1.1.2 Semantics of the Service Primitive. The primitive shall provide the following parameters:

PLS_DATA.request (OUTPUT_UNIT)

The OUTPUT_UNIT parameter can take on one of three values: ONE, ZERO, or DATA_COMPLETE and represent a single data bit. The DATA_COMPLETE value signifies that the Media Access Control sublayer has no more data to output.

6.3.1.1.3 When Generated. This primitive is generated by the MAC sublayer to request the transmission of a single data bit on the physical medium or to stop transmission.

6.3.1.1.4 Effect of Receipt. The receipt of this primitive will cause the PLS entity to encode and transmit either a single data bit or to cease transmission.

6.3.1.2 PLS_DATA.confirm

6.3.1.2.1 Function. This primitive has local significance and shall provide an appropriate response to the MAC sublayer PLS_DATA.request primitive.

6.3.1.2.2 Semantics of the Service Primitive. The semantics of this primitive are as follows:

PLS_DATA.confirm (OUTPUT_STATUS)

The OUTPUT_STATUS parameter can take one of two values: OUTPUT_ ABORT or OUTPUT_NEXT. The OUTPUT_ABORT value signifies that the PLS sublayer cannot complete the output request of sending a single bit on the medium. The OUTPUT_ABORT is available only when MAU is not available. The OUTPUT_NEXT value signifies that the PLS sublayer is ready for another PLS_DATA.request from the MAC sublayer.

6.3.1.2.3 When Generated. This primitive is generated in response to a PLS_DATA.request from the MAC sublayer.

6.3.1.2.4 Effect of Receipt. After receipt of this primitive by the MAC sublayer, additional PLS_DATA.request primitives can be generated by the MAC sublayer.

6.3.1.3 PLS_DATA.indicate

6.3.1.3.1 Function. This primitive defines the transfer of data from the PLS sublayer to the MAC sublayer.

6.3.1.3.2 Semantics of the Service Primitive. The semantics of the primitive are as follows:

PLS_DATA.indicate (INPUT_UNIT)

The INPUT_UNIT parameter can take one of two values each representing a single bit: ONE or ZERO.

6.3.1.3.3 When Generated. The PLS_DATA.indicate is generated to all MAC sublayer entities in the network after a PLS_DATA.request is issued.

NOTE: An indicate is also presented to the MAC entity that issued the request.

6.3.1.3.4 Effect of Receipt. The effect of receipt of this primitive by the MAC sublayer is unspecified.

6.3.2 Sublayer-to-Sublayer Service Primitives
6.3.2.1 PLS_CARRIER.indicate
6.3.2.1.1 Function. This primitive transfers the status of the activity on the physical medium from the PLS sublayer to the MAC sublayer.

6.3.2.1.2 Semantics of the Service Primitive. The semantics of the primitive are as follows:

PLS_CARRIER.indicate (CARRIER_STATUS)

The CARRIER_STATUS parameter can take one of two values: CARRIER_ON or CARRIER_OFF. The CARRIER_ON value indicates that the DTE Physical Layer had received an *input* message or a *signal_quality_ error* message from the MAU. The CARRIER_OFF value indicates that the DTE Physical Layer had received an *input_idle* message and is not receiving an SQE *signal_quality_error* message from the MAU.

6.3.2.1.3 When Generated. The PLS_CARRIER.indicate service primitive is generated whenever CARRIER_STATUS makes a transition from CARRIER_ON to CARRIER_OFF or vice versa.

6.3.2.1.4 Effect of Receipt. The effect of receipt of this primitive by the MAC sublayer is unspecified.

6.3.2.2 PLS_SIGNAL.indicate
6.3.2.2.1 Function. This primitive transfers the status of the Physical Layer signal quality from the PLS sublayer to the MAC sublayer.

6.3.2.2.2 Semantics of the Service Primitive. The semantics of the service primitive are as follows:

PLS_SIGNAL.indicate (SIGNAL_STATUS)

The SIGNAL_STATUS parameter can take one of two values: SIGNAL_ ERROR or NO_SIGNAL_ERROR. The SIGNAL_ERROR value indicates to the MAC sublayer that the PLS has received a *signal_quality_error* message from the MAU. The NO_SIGNAL_ERROR value indicates that the PLS has ceased to receive *signal_quality_error* messages from the MAU.

6.3.2.2.3 When Generated. The PLS_SIGNAL.indicate service primitive is generated whenever SIGNAL_STATUS makes a transition from SIGNAL_ERROR to NO_SIGNAL_ERROR or vice versa.

6.3.2.2.4 Effect of Receipt. The effect of receipt of this primitive by the MAC sublayer is unspecified.

7. Physical Signaling (PLS) and Attachment Unit Interface (AUI) Specifications

7.1 Scope. This section defines the logical, electrical, and mechanical characteristics for the PLS and AUI between Data Terminal Equipment and Medium Attachment Units used in CSMA/CD local area networks. The relationship of this specification to the entire IEEE Local Network standards is shown in Fig 7-1. The purpose of this interface is to provide an interconnection which is simple and inexpensive and which permits the development of simple and inexpensive MAUs.

This interface has the following characteristics:

(1) Capable of supporting one or more of the specified data rates

(2) Capable of driving up to 50 m (164 ft) of cable

(3) Permits the DTE to test the AUI, AUI cable, MAU, and the medium itself

(4) Supports MAUs for baseband coax, broadband coax, and baseband fiber

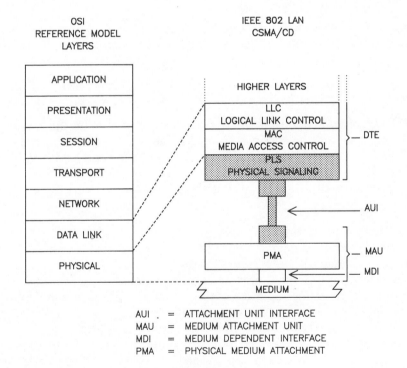

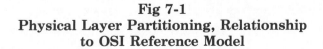

Fig 7-1
Physical Layer Partitioning, Relationship
to OSI Reference Model

7.1.1 Definitions

Attachment Unit Interface, AU Interface, AUI. The physical interface between the DTEs PLS sublayer and the MAUs Physical Medium Attachment (PMA) sublayer. The AUI carries encoded control and data signals.

BR. The rate of data throughput (bit rate) on the medium in bits per second.

bit time. The duration of one bit symbol (1/BR).

circuit. The physical medium on which signals are carried across the AUI. The data and control circuits consist of an A circuit and a B circuit forming a balanced transmission system so that the signal carried on the B circuit is the inverse of the signal carried on the A circuit.

Clocked Data One, CD1. A Manchester encoded data "1". A CD1 is encoded as a LO for the first half of the bit-cell and a HI for the second half of the bit-cell.

Clocked Data Zero, CD0. A Manchester encoded data "0". A CD0 is encoded as a HI for the first half of the bit-cell and a LO for the second half of the bit-cell.

Control Signal One, CS1. An encoded control signal used on the Control In and Control Out circuits. A CS1 is encoded as a signal at half the bit rate (BR/2).

Control Signal Zero, CS0. An encoded control signal used on the Control In and Control Out circuits. A CS0 is encoded as a signal at the bit rate (BR).

idle, IDL. A signal condition where no transition occurs on the transmission line is used to define the end of a frame and ceases to exist after the next LO to HI transition on the AUI circuits. An IDL always begins with a HI signal level. A driver is required to send the IDL signal for at least 2 bit times and a receiver is required to detect IDL within 1.6 bit times. See 7.3 for additional details.

7.1.2 Summary of Major Concepts

(1) Each direction of data transfer is serviced with two (making a total of four) balanced circuits: "Data" and "Control".

(2) The Data and Control circuits are independently self-clocked, thereby, eliminating the need for separate timing circuits. This is accomplished with encoding of all signals. The Control circuit signaling rate is nominally (but not of necessity exactly) equal to the Data circuit signaling rate.

(3) The Data circuits are used only for data transfer. No control signals associated with the interface are passed on these circuits. Likewise, the Control circuits are used only for control message transfer. No data signals associated with the interface are passed on these circuits.

7.1.3 Application. This standard applies to the interface used to interconnect Data Terminal Equipment (DTE) to a MAU that is not integrated as physical part of the DTE. This interface is used to:

(1) Provide the DTE with media independence for baseband coax, broadband coax, and baseband fiber media so that identical PLS, MAC, and LLC may be used with any of these media.

(2) Provide for the separation by cable of up to 50 m (164 ft) the DTE and the MAU.

7.1.4 Modes of Operation. The AUI can operate in two different modes. All interfaces shall support the normal mode. The monitor mode is optional.

When the interface is being operated in the *normal* mode, the AUI is logically connected to the MDI. The DTE is required to follow the media access algorithms, which provide a single access procedure compatible with all local area network media, to send data over the AUI. The MAU always sends back to the DTE whatever data the MAU receives on the MDI.

When the interface is in the optional *monitor* mode, the MAUs transmitter is logically isolated from the medium. The MAU, in this mode, functions as an observer on the medium. Both the input function and the signal quality error function are operational (see the MAU state diagrams for specific details).

7.1.5 Allocation of Function. The allocation of functions in the AUI is such that the majority of the functionality required by the interface can be provided by the DTE, leaving the MAU as simple as possible. This division of functions is based upon the recognition of the fact that since, in many cases, the MAU may be located in an inaccessible location adjacent to the physical medium, service of the MAU may often be difficult and expensive.

Explicit references on system components and test methods are given in Appendix A.

7.2 Functional Specification. The AUI is designed to make the differences among the various media as transparent as possible to the DTE. The selection of logical control signals and the functional procedures are all designed to this end. Figure 7-2 is a reference model, a generalized MAU as seen by the DTE through the AUI.

Many of the terms used in this section are specific to the interface between this sublayer and the MAC sublayer. These terms are defined in the Service Specification for the PLS sublayer.

7.2.1 PLS-PMA (DTE-MAU) Interface Protocol. The DTE and MAU communicate by means of a simple protocol across the AUI.

7.2.1.1 PLS to PMA Messages. The following messages can be sent by PLS sublayer entities in the DTE to PMA sublayer entities in the MAU:

Message	Meaning
output	Output information
output_idle	No data to be output
normal	Cease to Isolate the MAU
(Optional)	
isolate	Isolate MAU
mau_request	Request that the MAU be made available

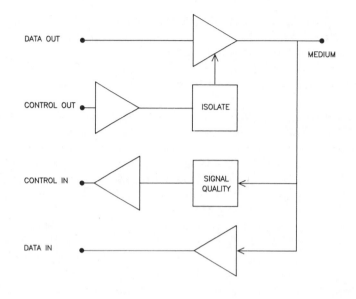

Fig 7-2
Generalized MAU Model

7.2.1.1.1 *output* message. The PLS sublayer sends an *output* message to the PMA sublayer when the PLS sublayer receives an OUTPUT_UNIT from the MAC sublayer.

The physical realization of the *output* message is a CD0 or a CD1 sent by the DTE to the MAU on the Data Out circuit. The DTE sends a CD0 if the OUTPUT_UNIT is a ZERO or a CD1 if the OUTPUT_UNIT is a ONE. This message is time coded — that is, once this message has been sent, the function is not completed over the AUI until one bit time later. The *output* message can not be sent again until the bit cell being sent as a result of sending the previous *output* message is complete.

7.2.1.1.2 *output_idle* message. The PLS sublayer sends an *output_ idle* message to the PMA sublayer at all times when the MAC sublayer is not in the process of transferring output data across the MAC to PLS interface. The *output_idle* message is no longer sent (and the first OUTPUT_UNIT is sent using the *output* message) as soon after the arrival of the first OUTPUT_UNIT as the MAU can be made available for data output. The *output_idle* message is again sent to the MAU when the DATA_COMPLETE is received from the MAC sublayer. The detailed usage of the *output_idle* message is shown in Fig 7-5.

The physical realization of the *output_idle* message is IDL sent by the DTE to the MAU on the Data Out circuit.

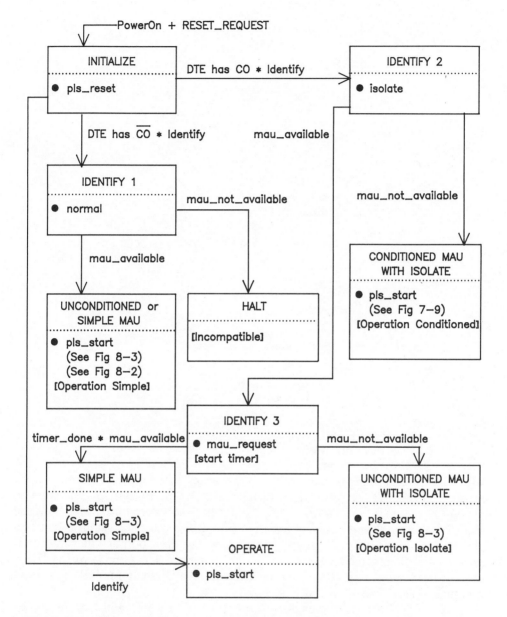

NOTES: (1) All states may be omitted except INITIALIZE and OPERATE
(2) "Identify" means DTE can recognize uniquely all CI messages and the entire function has been implemented
(3) "Identify" with bar means DTE fails to recognize *mau_not_available* or has a partial implementation of the function

Fig 7-3
PLS Reset and Identify Function

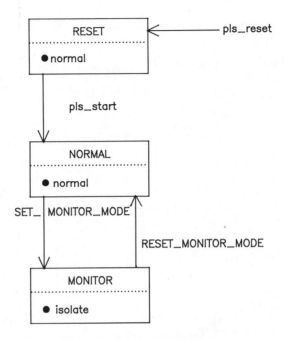

NOTE: Monitor State is optional

Fig 7-4
PLS Mode Function

7.2.1.1.3 *normal* message. The PLS sublayer sends a *normal* message to the PMA sublayer after it receives the PLS *start* message from the PLS Reset and Identify Function. The *normal* message is also sent after receipt of RESET_MONITOR_MODE from the management entity. The *normal* message is sent continuously by the PLS sublayer to the MAU, unless the PLS Output Function requires that the *mau_request* message be sent to permit data output. If *mau_request* is sent during data output, the sending of *normal* will be resumed when the PLS Output Function returns to the IDLE state. The *normal* signal is reset by the SET_MONITOR_MODE (this reset function is described more fully by Fig 7-4).

7.2.1.1.4 *isolate* message (Optional). The PLS sublayer sends an *isolate* message to the PMA (in the MAU) whenever the PLS sublayer receives SET_MONITOR_MODE from the management entity. In response to the *isolate* message, the MAU causes the means employed to impress data on the physical medium to be positively prevented from affecting the medium. Since signaling and isolation techniques differ from medium to medium, the manner in which this positive isolation of the transmitting means is accomplished is specified in the appropriate MAU section. However, the intent of this positive isolation of the transmitter is to ensure that the MAU will not interfere with the physical medium in such a way as to affect transmissions of other stations even in the event that the means normally employed to prevent the transmitter from affecting the medium have failed to do so. The specification of positive isolation is not to be construed to preclude use of either active or passive devices to accomplish this function.

The physical realization of the *isolate* message is a CS0 signal sent by the DTE to the MAU over the Control Out circuit.

7.2.1.1.5 *mau_request* message (Optional). The PLS sublayer sends the *mau_request* message to the PMA sublayer if the PMA sublayer is sending the *mau_not_available* message and the MAC sublayer has sent the first OUTPUT_UNIT of a new transmission. The PLS sublayer continues to send the *mau_request* message to the MAU until the MAC sublayer sends the DATA_COMPLETE request to the PLS sublayer across the MAC to PLS interface. See Figs 7-3, 7-5, and 7-9 for details.

In addition the *mau_request* message is used by the Reset and Identify Function in the IDENTIFY 3 state to determine whether the MAU has the Isolate Function.

The physical realization of *mau_request* is a CS1 sent by the DTE to the MAU on the Control Out circuit.

The physical realization of the *normal* message is the IDL signal sent by the DTE to the MAU on the Control Out circuit. In the absence of the CO circuit, MAUs implementing the Isolate Function shall act as if the *normal* message is present. The CO circuit components may be absent from the DTE, AUI, or MAU.

7.2.1.2 PMA to PLS Interface. The following messages can be sent by the Physical Medium Attachment sublayer entities in the MAU to the PLS sublayer entities in the DTE:

Message	Meaning
input	Input information
input_idle	No input information
signal_quality_error	Error detected by MAU
mau_available	MAU is available for output
(Optional)	
mau_not_available	MAU is not available for output

7.2.1.2.1 *input* message. The PMA sublayer sends an *input* message to the PLS sublayer when the MAU has received a bit from the medium and is prepared to transfer this bit to the DTE. The actual mapping of the signals on the medium to the type of *input* message to be sent to the DTE is contained in the specifications for each specific MAU type. In general, when the *signal_quality_error* message is being sent by the MAU, the symmetry specifications for circuit DI are not guaranteed to be met.

The physical realization of the *input* message consists of CD0 or CD1 waveforms. If the *signal_quality_error* message is being sent from the MAU, the input waveform is unpredictable.

NOTE: This signal is not necessarily retimed by the MAU. Consult the appropriate MAU specification for timing and jitter.

7.2.1.2.2 *input_idle* **message.** The PMA sublayer sends an *input_idle* message to the PLS sublayer when the MAU does not have data to send to the DTE.

The physical realization of the *input_idle* message is an IDL sent by the MAU to the DTE on the Data In circuit.

7.2.1.2.3 *signal_quality_error* **message.** The PMA sublayer sends a *signal_quality_error* message to the PLS sublayer in response to any of three possible conditions. These conditions are: improper signals on the medium, collision on the medium, and reception of the *output_idle* message. They are described in the following numbered paragraphs. The physical realization of the *signal_quality* error message is a CS0 sent by the MAU to the DTE on the Control In circuit.

NOTE: The MAU is required to assert the *signal_quality_error* message at the appropriate times whenever the MAU is powered, and not just when the DTE is requesting data output. See Figs 7-9, 8-2, and 8-3 for details.

(1) *Improper Signals on the Medium.* The MAU may send the *signal_quality_error* message at any time due to improper signals on the medium. The exact nature of these improper signals are medium dependent. Typically, this condition might be caused by a malfunctioning MAU (for example, repeater or head-end) connected to the medium or by a break or short in the medium. See the appropriate MAU specification for specific conditions that may cause improper signals on a given medium.

(2) Collision. Collision occurs when more than one MAU is transmitting on the medium. The local MAU shall send the *signal_quality_error* message in every instance when it is possible for it to ascertain that more than one MAU is transmitting on the medium. The MAU shall make the best determination possible. The MAU shall not send the *signal_quality_error* message when it is unable to determine conclusively that more than one MAU is transmitting.

(3) *signal_quality_error* message Test. The MAU sends the *signal_quality_error* message at the completion of the Output Function. See Fig 7-9 and Section 8 for a more complete description of this test.

7.2.1.2.4 *mau_available* **message.** The PMA sublayer sends the *mau_available* message to the PLS sublayer when the MAU is available for output. The *mau_available* message is always sent by a MAU that is always prepared to output data except when it is required to signal the *signal_quality_error* message. Such a MAU does not require *mau_request* to prepare itself for data output. See Figs 7-3, 7-5, and 7-9 for details.

The physical realization of the *mau_available* message is an IDL sent by the MAU to the DTE on the Control In circuit.

7.2.1.2.5 *mau_not_available* **message** (Optional). The PMA sublayer sends a *mau_not_available* message to the PLS sublayer when the MAU is not available for output. Figure 7-5 shows the relationship of *mau_not_available* to the Output Function.

The *mau_not_available* message is also used by a MAU that contains the Isolate Function and does not need to be conditioned for output to signal the presence of the Isolate Function during the PLS Reset Function (See Figs 7-3 and 8-3).

The physical realization of the *mau_not_available* message is a CS1 sent by the MAU to the DTE on the Control In circuit.

7.2.2 PLS Interface to MAC and Management Entities. The PLS sublayer interfaces described here are for reference only. This section specifies the services sent between the MAC sublayer and the PLS sublayer.

7.2.2.1 PLS-MAC Interface. The following messages can be sent between PLS sublayer entities and MAC sublayer entities:

Message	Meaning
OUTPUT_UNIT	Data sent to the MAU
OUTPUT_STATUS	Response to OUTPUT_UNIT
INPUT_UNIT	Data received from the MAU
CARRIER_STATUS	Indication of input activity
SIGNAL_STATUS	Indication of error/no error condition

7.2.2.1.1 OUTPUT_UNIT. The MAC sublayer sends the PLS sublayer an OUTPUT_UNIT every time the MAC sublayer has a bit to send. Once the MAC sublayer has sent an OUTPUT_UNIT to the PLS sublayer, it may not send another OUTPUT_UNIT until it has received an OUTPUT_STATUS message from the PLS sublayer. The OUTPUT_UNIT is a ONE if the MAC sublayer wants the PLS sublayer to send a CD1 to the PMA sublayer, a ZERO if a CD0 is desired, or a DATA_COMPLETE if an IDL is desired.

7.2.2.1.2 OUTPUT_STATUS. The PLS sublayer OUTPUT_STATUS in response to every OUTPUT_UNIT received by the PLS sublayer. OUTPUT_STATUS sent is an OUTPUT_NEXT if the PLS sublayer is ready to accept the next OUTPUT_UNIT from the MAC sublayer, or an OUTPUT_ABORT if the PLS sublayer was not able to process the previous OUTPUT_UNIT. (The purpose of OUTPUT—STATUS is to synchronize the MAC sublayer data output with the data rate of the physical medium.)

7.2.2.1.3 INPUT_UNIT. The PLS Sublayer sends the MAC sublayer an INPUT_UNIT every time the PLS receives an *input* message from the PMA sublayer. The INPUT_UNIT is a ONE if the PLS sublayer receives a CD1 from the PMA sublayer, a ZERO if the PLS sublayer receives a CD0 from the PMA sublayer.

7.2.2.1.4 CARRIER_STATUS. The PLS sublayer sends the MAC sublayer CARRIER_STATUS whenever the PLS sublayer detects a change in carrier status. The PLS sublayer sends CARRIER_ON when it receives an *input* or *signal_quality_error* message from the PMA and the previous CARRIER_STATUS that the PLS sublayer sent to the MAC sublayer was CARRIER_OFF. The PLS sublayer sends CARRIER_OFF when it receives an *input_idle* from the PMA sublayer, no *signal_quality_error* (either *mau_available* or *mau_not_available*) message and the previous CARRIER_STATUS that the PLS sublayer sent to the MAC sublayer was CARRIER_ON.

7.2.2.1.5 SIGNAL_STATUS. The PLS sublayer sends the MAC sublayer SIGNAL_STATUS whenever the PLS sublayer detects a change in the signal quality (as reported by the PMA). The PLS sublayer sends SIGNAL_ERROR when it receives a *signal_quality_error* message from the PMA sublayer and the previous SIGNAL_STATUS the PLS sublayer sent was NO_SIGNAL_ERROR. The PLS sublayer sends NO_SIGNAL_ERROR when it receives no *signal_quality_error* (either *mau_available* or *mau_not_available*) message from the PMA sublayer and the previous CARRIER_STATUS that the PLS sent to the MAC sublayer was SIGNAL_ERROR.

7.2.2.2 PLS-Management Entity Interface. The following messages may be sent between the PLS sublayer entities and intralayer or higher layer management entities:

Message	Meaning
RESET_REQUEST	Reset PLS to initial "Power On" state
RESET_RESPONSE	Provides operational information
MODE_CONTROL	Control operation
SQE_TEST	Signal Quality Error test results

7.2.2.2.1 RESET_REQUEST. The management entity sends the PLS sublayer RESET_REQUEST when the PLS sublayer needs to be reset to a known state. Upon receipt of RESET_REQUEST, the PLS sublayer resets all internal logic and restarts all functions. See Fig 7-3 for details.

7.2.2.2.2 RESET_RESPONSE. The PLS sublayer sends the management entity RESET_RESPONSE upon completion of the Reset and Identify Function (see Fig 7-3 and 7.2.4.1) whether invoked due to power on or due to a RESET_REQUEST. Which RESET_RESPONSE was sent is determined by the Reset and Identify Function. A RESET_RESPONSE of OPERATION SIMPLE, OPERATION ISOLATE, or OPERATION CONDITIONED is sent if the MAU is compatible with the DTE and the MAU is simple (no isolate) or if the DTE does not support Isolate even if Isolate is supported by the MAU, supports Isolate but does not require conditioning, or supports Isolate and does require conditioning to output. A RESET_RESPONSE of INCOMPATIBLE is sent if the MAU is not compatible with the DTE (that is, the MAU requires conditioning but the DTE does not support conditioning).

7.2.2.2.3 MODE_CONTROL. The management entity sends MODE_
CONTROL to the PLS sublayer to control PLS functions. MODE_CONTROL
capabilities are:

Message	Meaning
ACTIVATE_PHYSICAL	Supply power on circuit VP
DEACTIVATE_PHYSICAL	Remove power fron circuit VP
SET_MONITOR_MODE	Send Isolate to MAU
RESET_MONITOR_MODE	Send Normal to MAU

7.2.2.2.4 SQE_TEST. The PLS sublayer sends SQE_TEST to the
management entity at the conclusion of each *signal_quality_error* test (see
Output Function, 7.2.4.3). The PLS sublayer sends SQE_TEST_ERROR if the
signal_quality_error test fails or SQE_TEST_OK if the *signal_quality_error*
test passes.

7.2.3 Frame Structure. Frames transmitted on the AUI shall have the
following structure:

<silence><preamble><sfd><data><etd><silence>

The frame elements shall have the following characteristics:

Element	Characteristics
<silence>	= no transitions
<preamble>	= alternating (CD1) and (CD0) >= 56 bit times (ending in CD0)
<sfd>	= (CD1)(CD0)(CD1)(CD0)(CD1)(CD0)(CD1)(CD1)
<data>	= $8 \times N$
<etd>	= IDL

7.2.3.1 Silence. The <silence> delimiter provides an observation
window for an unspecified period of time during which no transitions occur
on the AUI. The minimum length of this period is specified by the access
procedure.

7.2.3.2 Preamble. The <preamble> delimiter begins a frame transmission and provides a signal for receiver synchronization. The signal shall be an
alternating pattern of (CD1) and (CD0). This pattern shall be transmitted on
the Data Out circuit by the DTE to the MAU for a minimum of 56 bit times at
the beginning of each frame. The last bit of the preamble (that is, the final bit
of preamble before the start of frame delimiter) shall be a CD0.

The DTE is required to supply at least 56 bits of preamble in order to satisfy
system requirements. System components consume preamble bits in order to
perform their functions. The number of preamble bits sourced ensures an
adequate number of bits are provided to each system component to correctly
implement its function.

7.2.3.3 Start of Frame Delimiter. The sfd indicates the start of a frame, and follows the preamble. The sfd element of a frame shall be:

(CD1)(CD0)(CD1)(CD0)(CD1)(CD0)(CD1)(CD1)

7.2.3.4 Data. The data in a transmission shall be in multiples of eight (8) encoded data bits (CD0s and CD1s).

7.2.3.5 End of Transmission Delimiter. The <etd> delimiter indicates the end of a transmission and serves to turn off the transmitter. The signal shall be an IDL.

7.2.4 PLS Functions. The PLS sublayer functions consist of a Reset and Identify Function and five simultaneous and asynchronous functions. These function are Output, Input, Mode, Error Sense, and Carrier Sense. All of the five functions are started immediately following the completion of the Reset and Identify Function.

These functions are depicted in the state diagrams shown in Figs 7-3, 7-4, 7-5, 7-6, 7-7, and 7-8. State names are shown in capital letters in the enclosed areas at the top of each state box. Message names and actions are given in both capital and lower-case letters. Labels on transitions are qualifiers that must be fulfilled before the transition will be taken. Actions described by short descriptive phrases are enclosed by parentheses. State transitions and sending and receiving of messages occur instantaneously. When a state is entered, and the condition to leave that state is not immediately fulfilled, the state executes continuously, sending the messages and executing the actions contained in the state in a continuous manner. The state diagrams contain the authoritative statement of the intended functions, and when apparent conflicts between descriptive text and the state diagrams arise, the state diagrams are to take precedence.

7.2.4.1 Reset and Identify Function. The Reset and Identify Function is executed any time either of two conditions occur. These two conditions are "power on" and the receipt of RESET_REQUEST from the management entity. The Reset and Identify Function initializes all PLS functions, and (optionally) determines the cabability of the MAU attached to the AUI. Figure 7-3 is the state diagram of the Reset and Identify Function. The Identify portion of the function is optional.

7.2.4.2 Mode Function. The MAU functions in two modes, normal and monitor. The monitor mode is optional. The state diagram of Fig 7-4 depicts the operation of the Mode Function. When the MAU is operating in the normal mode, it functions as a direct connection between the DTE and the medium. Data sent from the DTE is impressed onto the medium by the MAU and all data appearing on the medium is sent to the DTE by the MAU. When the MAU is operating in the monitor mode, data appearing on the medium is sent to the DTE by the MAU as during the normal mode. *signal_quality_error* is also asserted on the AUI as during operation in the normal mode. However,

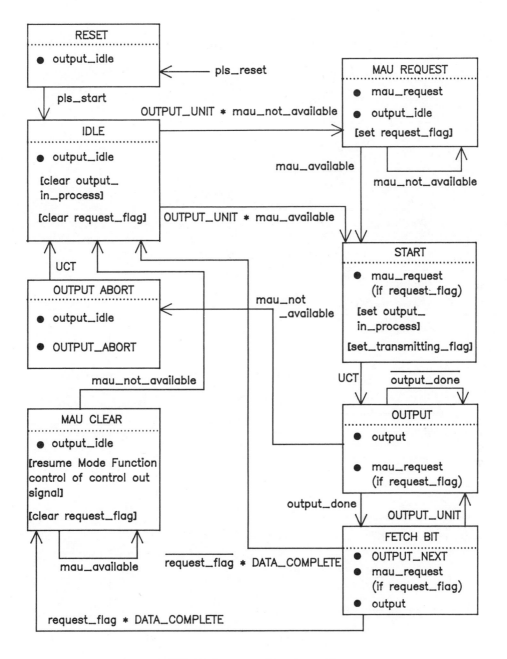

NOTE: UCT = unconditional transition

**Fig 7-5
PLS Output Function**

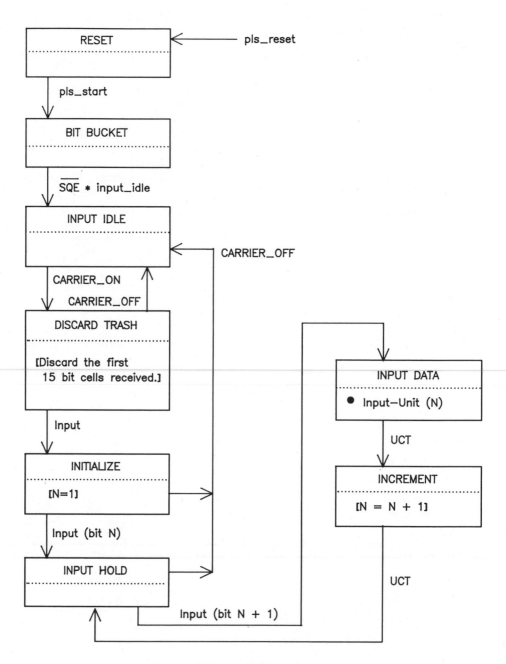

NOTE: UCT= unconditional transition

**Figure 7-6
PLS Input Function**

in the monitor mode, the means employed to impress data on the physical medium is positively prevented from affecting the medium. Since signaling and isolation techniques differ from medium to medium, the manner in which this positive isolation of the transmitting means is accomplished is specified in the appropriate MAU document. However, the intent of this positive isolation of the transmitter is to ensure that the MAU will not interfere with the physical medium in such a way as to affect transmission of other stations even in the event of failure of the normal transmitter disabling control paths within the transmitting mechanism of the MAU.

The monitor mode is intended to permit a network station to determine if it is the source of interference observed on the medium.

NOTE: The monitor mode is intended to be used only by Network Management for fault isolation and network operation verification. It is intended that the *isolate* message provide direct control over the mode function so that these tasks can be performed. IMPROPER USE OF THE ISOLATE FUNCTION CAN CAUSE ERRONEOUS FRAMES. The section on Network Management will provide details on the proper use of this function.

7.2.4.3 Output Function. The PLS sublayer Output Function transparently performs the tasks of conditioning the MAU for output, (*mau_request*, *mau_available* handshake) and data transfer from the MAC sublayer to the MAU. The state diagram of Fig 7-5 depicts the Output Function operation.

At the conclusion of the Output Function, if a collision has not occurred, a test is performed to verify operation of the signal quality detection mechanism in the MAU and to verify the ability of the AUI to pass the *signal_quality_error* message to the PLS sublayer. The operation of this test in the DTE is shown in Fig 7-8.

7.2.4.4 Input Function. The PLS sublayer Input Function transparently performs the task of data transfer from the MAU to the MAC sublayer. The state diagram of Fig 7-6 depicts the Input Function operation.

7.2.4.5 Error Sense Function. The PLS sublayer Error Sense Function performs the task of sending SIGNAL_STATUS to the MAC sublayer whenever there is a change in the signal quality information received from the MAU. The state diagram of Fig 7-7 depicts the Error Sense Function operation.

7.2.4.6 Carrier Sense Function. The PLS sublayer Carrier Sense Function performs the task of sending CARRIER_STATUS to the MAC sublayer every time there is a change in CARRIER_STATUS. The state diagram of Fig 7-8 depicts the Carrier Sense Function operation.

Verification of the *signal_quality_error* detection mechanism occurs in the following manner (in the absence of a fault on the medium).

(1) At the conclusion of the output function, the DTE opens a time window during which it expects to see the *signal_quality_error* signal asserted on the Control In circuit. The time window begins when CARRIER_STATUS becomes CARRIER_OFF. If execution of the Output Function does not cause CARRIER_ON to occur no SQE test occurs in the DTE. The duration of the

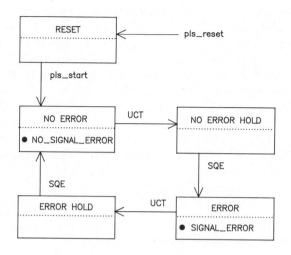

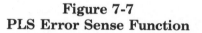

NOTE: UCT= unconditional transition

Figure 7-7
PLS Error Sense Function

window shall be at least 4.0 μs but no more than 8.0 μs. During the time window (depicted as carrier—inhibit—timer, Fig 7-8) the Carrier Sense Function is inhibited.

(2) The MAU, upon waiting Tw after the conclusion of output, activates as much of the signal quality error detecting mechanism as is possible without placing signals on the medium, thus sending the *signal_quality_error* message across the AUI for 10 ± 5 bit times (10/BR ± 5/BR seconds).

(3) The DTE interprets the reception of the *signal_quality_error* message from the MAU as indication that the *signal_quality_error* detecting mechanism is operational and the *signal_quality_error* message may be both sent by the MAU and received by the DTE.

NOTES: (1) The occurrence of multiple (overlapping) transmitters on the medium during the time that the test window is open, as specified above, will satisfy the test and will verify proper operation of the signal quality error detecting mechanism and sending and receiving of the appropriate physical error message.

(2) If signal_quality_error exists at the DTE before CARRIER_OFF occurs, then the Collision Presence test sequence within the PLS as described in 7.2.4.3 above shall be aborted as shown in Fig 7-8.

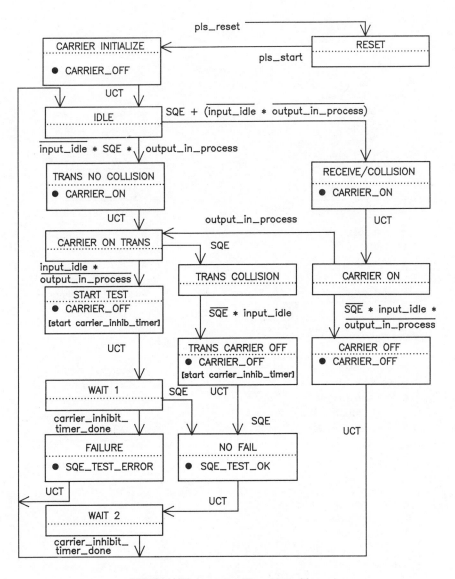

NOTE: UCT = unconditional transition
SQE = *signal_quality_error*

Fig 7-8
PLS Carrier Sense Function

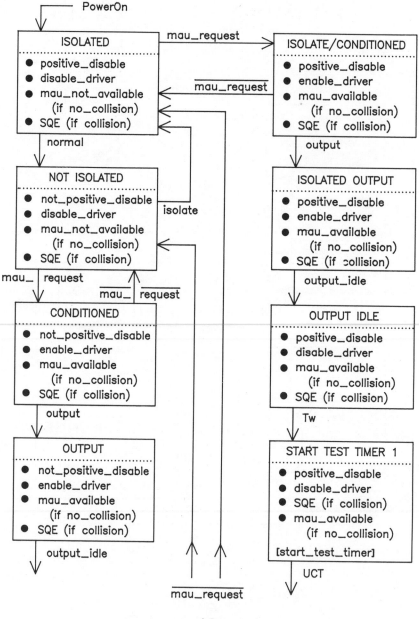

(a)

NOTE: See Figs 8-2 and 8-3 for simple and isolate type MAUs.

Fig 7-9
Interface Function for MAU with Conditioning

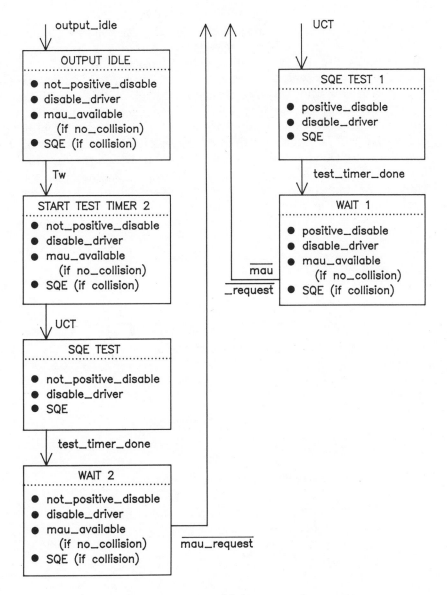

(b)

NOTE: See Figs 8-2 and 8-3 for simple and isolate type MAUs.

Fig 7-9
Interface Function for MAU with Conditioning

7.3 Signal Characteristics

7.3.1 Signal Encoding. Two different signal encoding mechanisms may be used by the AUI. One of the mechanisms is used to encode data, the other to encode control. The control encoding is for future study.

7.3.1.1 Data Encoding. Manchester encoding is used for the transmission of data across the AUI. Manchester encoding is a binary signaling mechanism that combines data and clock into "bit-symbols". Each bit-symbol is split into two halves with the second half containing the binary inverse of the first half; a transition always occurs in the middle of each bit-symbol. During the first half of the bit-symbol, the encoded signal is the logical complement of the bit value being encoded. During the second half of the bit-symbol, the encoded signal is the uncomplemented value of the bit being encoded. Thus, a CD0 is encoded as a bit-symbol in which the first half is HI and the second half is LO. A CD1 is encoded as a bit-symbol in which the first half is LO and the second half is HI. Examples of Manchester waveforms are shown in Fig 7-10.

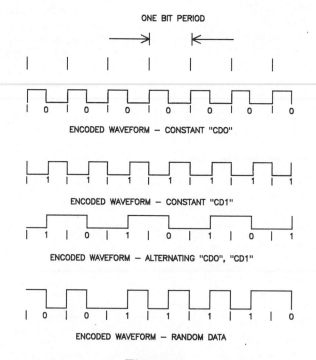

**Fig 7-10
Examples of Manchester Waveforms**

The line condition IDL is also used as an encoded signal. An IDL always starts with a HI signal level. Since IDL always starts with a HI signal, an additional transition will be added to the data stream if the last bit sent was a zero. This transition can not be confused with clocked data (CD0 or CD1) since the transition will occur at the start of a bit cell. There will be no transition in the middle of the bit cell. The IDL condition, as sent by a driver, shall be maintained for a minimum of 2 bit times. The IDL condition shall be detected within 1.6 bit times at the receiving device.

(1) System jitter considerations make detection of IDL (etd, end transmission delimiter) earlier than 1.3 bit times impractical. The specific implementation of the phase-locked loop or equivalent clock recovery mechanism determines the lower bound on the actual IDL detection time. Adequate margin between lower bound and 1.6 bit times should be considered.

(2) Recovery of timing implicit in the data is easily accomplished at the receiving side of the interface because of the wealth of binary transitions guaranteed to be in the encoded waveform, independent of the data sequence. A phase-locked loop or equivalent mechanism maintains continuous tracking of the phase of the information on the Data circuit.

7.3.1.2 Control Encoding. A simpler encoding mechanism is used for control signaling than for data signaling. The encoded symbols used in this signaling mechanism are CS0, CS1, and IDL. The CS0 signal is a signal stream of frequency equal to the bit rate (BR). The CS1 signal is a signal stream of frequency equal to half of the bit rate (BR/2). If the interface supports more then one bit rate (see 4.2), the bit rate in use on the data circuits is the one to which the control signals are referenced. The IDL signal used on the control circuits is the same as the IDL signal defined for the data circuits (see 7.3.1.1). The Control Out circuit is optional (0) as is one message on Control In. The tolerance on CO is BR $\pm$ 5% and on CI it is BR $\pm$ 15%. The nominal duty cycle is 50/50 and shall be no worse than 60/40.

The meaning of the signals on the Control Out circuit (DTE to MAU) are:

Signal	Message		Description
IDL	normal		Instructs the MAU to enter (remain in) normal mode
CS1	mau_request (O)		Requests that the MAU should be made available
CS0	isolate	(O)	Instructs the MAU to enter (remain in) monitor mode

The meaning of the signals on the Control In circuit (MAU to DTE) are:

Signal	Message	Description
IDL	mau_available	Indicates that the MAU is ready to output data
CS1	mau_not_available (O)	Indicates that the MAU is not ready to output data
CS0	signal_quality_error	Indicates that the MAU has detected an error on input data

81

7.3.2 Signaling Rate. Signaling rates of from 1 to 20 Mb/s are encompassed by this standard. This edition of the standard specifies a signaling rate of 10 million bits per second ± 0.01%.

It is intended that a given MDI operate at a single data rate. It is not precluded that specific DTE and MAU designs be manually switched or set to alternate rates. A given local network shall operate at a single signaling rate. To facilitate the configuration of operational systems, DTE and MAU devices shall be labeled with the actual signaling rate used with that device.

7.3.3 Signaling Levels. Exact voltage and current specifications are listed in 7-4.

7.4 Electrical Characteristics. Terms BR and BR/2 have very specific meaning as used in this subsection. The term BR is used to mean the bit rate of the highest signaling rate supported by any one implementation of this interface, BR/2 is used to mean half the bit rate of the lowest signaling rate supported by any one implementation of this interface (see 7.3.2). An interface may support one or more signaling rates.

NOTE: The characteristics of the driver and receiver can be achieved with standard ECL logic with the addition of an appropriate coupling network, however this implementation is not mandatory.

7.4.1 Driver Characteristics. The driver is a differential driver capable of driving the specified 78 Ω interface cable. Only the parameters necessary to ensure compatibility with the specified receiver and to assure personnel safety at the interface connector are specified in the following sections.

7.4.1.1 Differential Output Voltage, Loaded. Drivers shall meet all requirements of this section under *two* basic sets of test conditions (that is, each of two resistive values). For drivers located within a DTE, a combined inductive load of 27 μH, ± 1% and either a 73 Ω or 83 Ω ± 1% resistive load shall be used. For a driver located within a MAU, a combined inductive load of 50 μH, ± 1% and either 73 Ω or 83 Ω ± 1% resistive load shall be used.

The differential output voltage, V_{dm}, is alternately positive and negative in magnitude with respect to zero voltage. The value of V_{dm} into either of the two test loads identified above (R = 73 Ω or 83 Ω, ± 1%) at the interface connector of the driving unit shall satisfy the conditions defined by values V_1, V_2, and V_3 shown in Fig 7-12 for signals in between BR and BR/2 meeting the frequency and duty cycle tolerances specified for the signal being driven. The procedure for measuring and applying the test condition is as follows:

(1) Measure the output voltage V_{dm} for the driver being tested at the waveform point after overshoot, before droop, under test load conditions of 7.4.1.1. This voltage is V_2.

(2) Calculate V_1 and V_3

(3) V_1 shall be < 1315 mV, V_3 shall be > 450 mV

(4) The waveform shall remain within shaded area limits

The differential output voltage magnitude, V_{dm}, into either of the two test

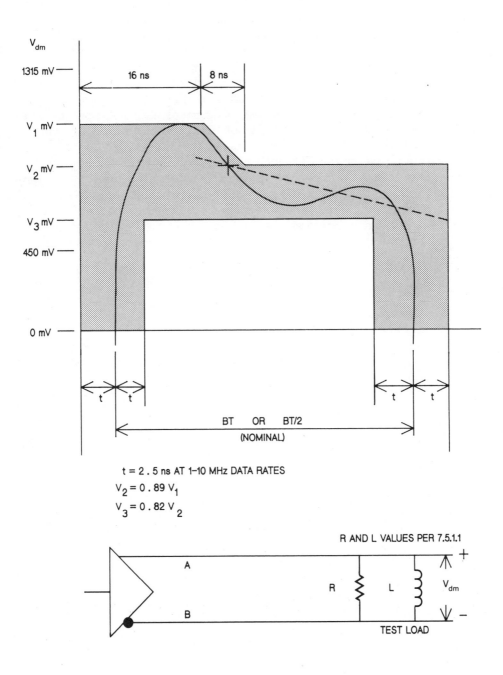

$t = 2.5$ ns AT 1–10 MHz DATA RATES

$V_2 = 0.89 V_1$

$V_3 = 0.82 V_2$

**Fig 7-11
Differential Output Voltage, Loaded**

loads identified above, at the interface connector of the driving unit during the idle state shall be within 40 mV of 0 V. The current into either of the two test loads shall be limited to 4 mA.

When a driver, connected to the appropriate two test loads identified above, enters the idle state, it shall maintain a minimum differential output voltage of at least $0.7 \cdot V_2$ mV for at least 2 bit times after the last low to high transition. The driver differential output voltage shall then approach within 40 mV of 0 V within 80 bit times. In addition, the current into the appropriate test load shall be limited in magnitude to 4 mA within 80 bit times. Undershoot, if any, upon reaching 0 V shall be limited to –100 mV. See Fig 7-11.

For drivers on either the CO or CI circuits, the first transition or the last positive going transition may occur asynchronously with respect to the timing of the following transitions or the preceeding transition(s), respectively.

The receiving unit shall take precautions to ensure that a HI to idle transition is not falsely interpreted as an idle to nonidle transition, even in the presence of signal droop due to ac coupling in the interface driver or receiver circuits.

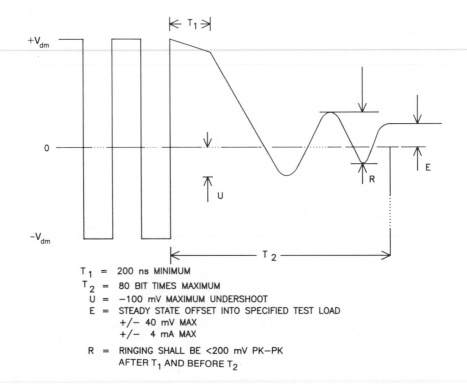

T_1 = 200 ns MINIMUM
T_2 = 80 BIT TIMES MAXIMUM
U = −100 mV MAXIMUM UNDERSHOOT
E = STEADY STATE OFFSET INTO SPECIFIED TEST LOAD
+/− 40 mV MAX
+/− 4 mA MAX

R = RINGING SHALL BE <200 mV PK−PK
AFTER T_1 AND BEFORE T_2

Fig 7-12
Generalized Driver Waveform

When the driver becomes nonidle after a period of idle on the interface circuit, the differential output voltage at the interface connector shall meet the requirements of 7.4.1.1 beginning with the first bit transmitted. The first transition may occur asynchronously with respect to the timing of the following transitions.

7.4.1.3 AC Common Mode Output Voltage. The magnitude of the ac component of the common mode output voltage of the driver, measured between the midpoint of a test load consisting of a pair of matched 39 Ω ± 1% resistors and circuit V_C, as shown in Fig 7-13, shall not exceed 40 mV peak.

7.4.1.4 Differential Output Voltage, Open Circuit. The differential output voltage into an open circuit, measured at the interface connector of the driving unit, shall not exceed 13 V peak.

7.4.1.5 DC Common Mode Output Voltage. The magnitude of the dc component of the common mode output voltage of the driver, measured between the midpoint of a test load consisting of a pair of matched 39 Ω ± 1% resistors and circuit V_C, as shown in Fig 7-13, shall not exceed 5.5 V.

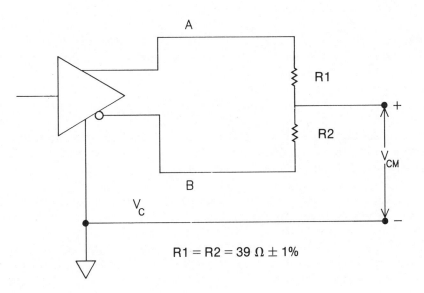

Fig 7-13
Common Mode Output Voltage

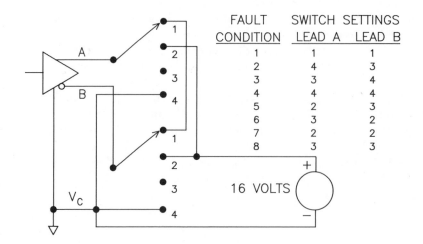

Fig 7-14
Driver Fault Conditions

7.4.1.6 Fault Tolerance. Any single driver in the interface, when idle or driving any permissible signal, shall tolerate the application of each of the faults specified by the switch settings in Fig 7-14 indefinitely; and after the fault condition is removed, the operation of the driver, according to the specifications of 7.4.1.1 through 7.4.1.5, shall not be impaired.

In addition, the magnitude of the output current from either output of the driver under any of the fault conditions specified shall not exceed 150 mA.

7.4.2 Receiver Characteristics. The receiver specified terminates the interface cable in its characteristic impedance. The receiver shall function normally over the specified dc and ac common mode ranges.

7.4.2.1 Receiver Threshold Levels. When the receiving interface circuit at the interface connector of the receiving equipment is driven by a differential input signal at either BR or BR/2 meeting the frequency and duty cycle tolerances specified for the receiving circuit, when the A lead is 160 mV positive with respect to the B lead, the interface circuit is in the HI state, and when the A lead is 160 mV negative with respect to the B lead, the interface circuit is in the LO state. The receiver output shall assume the intended HI and LO states for the corresponding input conditions.

NOTE: The specified threshold levels do not take precedence over the duty cycle and jitter tolerance specified elsewhere. Both sets of specifications must be met.

7.4.2.2 AC Differential Input Impedance. The ac differential input impedance for AUI receivers located in MAUs shall have a real part of 77.83 Ω ± 6%, with the sign of the imaginary part positive, and the phase angle of the impedance in degrees ≤ 0.0338 times the real part of the impedance, when measured with a 10 MHz sine wave.

The ac differential input impedance AUI receivers located in the DTE shall have a real part of 77.95 Ω ± 6%, with the sign of the imaginary part positive, and the phase angle of the impedance in degrees ≤ 0.0183 times the real part of the impedance, when measured with a 10 MHz sine wave.

A 78 Ω ± 6% resistor in parallel with an inductance of greater than 27 μH or 50 μH for receivers in the MAU and DTE respectively, satisfies this requirement.

7.4.2.3 AC Common Mode Range. When the receiving interface circuit at the receiving equipment is driven by a differential input signal at either BR or BR/2 meeting the frequency and duty cycle tolerances specified for the circuit being driven, the receiver output shall assume the proper output state as specified in 7.4.2.1, in the presence of a peak common mode ac sine wave voltage either of from 30 Hz to 40 kHz referenced to circuit V_C in magnitude from 0 to 3 V, or in magnitude 0 to 100 mV for ac voltages of from 40 kHz to BR as shown in Fig 7-15.

NOTE: The receiver shall also be able to reject small ac common mode signals in frequencies outside of this range.

7.4.2.4 Total Common Mode Range. When the receiving interface circuit at the receiving equipment is driven by a differential input signal at either BR or BR/2 meeting the frequency and duty cycle tolerances specified for the circuit being driven, the receiver output shall assume the intended output state as specified in 7.4.2.1 in the presence of a total common mode voltage, dc plus ac, referenced to circuit V_C in magnitude from 0 to 5.5 V, as shown in the test setup of Fig 7-15. The AC component shall not exceed the requirements of 7.4.2.3.

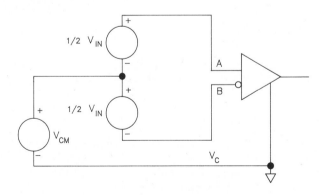

Fig 7-15
Common Mode Input Test

The receiver shall be so designed that the magnitude of the current from the common mode voltage source used in the test shall not exceed 1 mA.

7.4.2.5 Requirements after Idle. When the receiver becomes nonidle after a period of idle on the interface circuit, the characteristics of the signal at the output of the receiver shall stabilize within the startup delay allowed for the device incorporating the receiver so that it is not prevented from meeting the jitter specifications established for that device.

7.4.2.6 Fault Tolerance. Any single receiver in the interface shall tolerate the application of each of the faults specified by the switch settings in Fig 7-16 indefinitely, and after the fault condition is removed, the operation of the receiver according to the specifications of 7.4.2.1 through 7.4.2.6 shall not be impaired.

In addition, the magnitude of the current into either input of the receiver under any of the fault conditions specified shall not exceed 3 mA.

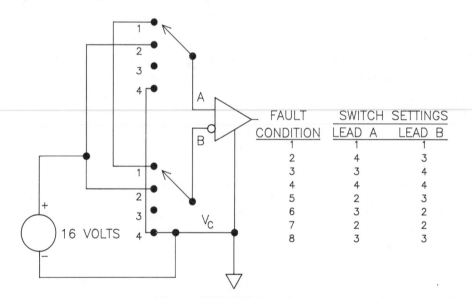

FAULT CONDITION	SWITCH SETTINGS LEAD A	LEAD B
1	1	1
2	4	3
3	3	4
4	4	4
5	2	3
6	3	2
7	2	2
8	3	3

Fig 7-16
Receiver Fault Conditions

7.4.3 AUI Cable Characteristics. The interface cable consists of individually shielded twisted pairs of wires with an overall shield covering these individual shielded wire pairs. These shields must provide sufficient shielding to meet the requirements of protection against rf interference and the following cable parameters. Individual shields for each signal pair are electrically isolated from the outer shield but not necessarily from each other.

The overall shield shall be returned to the MAU and DTE Units via the AUI connector shell as defined in 7.6.2 and 7.6.3. If a common drain wire is used for all the signal pair shields, then it shall be connected to pin 4. Individual drain wire returns for each signal pair may be used (see 7.6.3). It is recommended that individual drain wires be used on all control and data circuit shields to meet satisfactory crosstalk levels. If individual drain wires are used, they shall be interconnected within the AUI cable at each end and shall be connected at least to pin 4 at each end of the cable.

The presence of the Control Out signal pair is optional. If driver or receiver circuit components for CO are not provided, consideration should be given to properly terminating the CO signal pair within the DTE and MAU to preclude erroneous operation.

7.4.3.1 Conductor Size. The dc power pair in the interconnecting cable, voltage plus and voltage minus, shall be composed of a twisted pair of sufficient gauge stranded wires to result in a nominal dc resistance not to exceed 1.75 Ω per conductor.

Conductor size for the signal pairs shall be determined according to the ac related parameters in 6.5.3.2–6.5.3.6.

7.4.3.2 Pair-to-Pair Balanced Crosstalk. The balanced crosstalk from one pair of wires to any other pair in the same cable sheath (when each pair is driven per 7.4.1.1–7.4.1.5) shall have a minimum value of 40 dB of attenuation measured over the range of BR/2 to BR.

7.4.3.3 Differential Characteristic Impedance. The differential characteristic impedance for all pairs shall be equal within 3 Ω and shall be 78 $\pm$ 5 Ω measured at a frequency of BR.

7.4.3.4 Transfer Impedance. (1) The common mode transfer impedance shall not exceed the values shown in Fig 7-17 over the indicated frequency range.

(2) The differential mode transfer impedance for all pairs shall be at least 20 dB below the common mode transfer impedance.

7.4.3.5 Attenuation. Total cable attenuation levels between driver and receiver (at separate stations) for each signal pair shall not exceed 3 dB over the frequency range of BR/2 to BR (Hz) for sine-wave measurements.

7.4.3.6 Timing Jitter. Cable meeting this specification shall exhibit edge jitter of no more than 1.5 ns at the receiving end when the longest legal length of the cable as specified in 7.4.3.1 through 7.4.3.7 is terminated in a 78 Ω $\pm$ 1% resistor at the receiving end and is driven with pseudorandom Manchester encoded binary data from a data generator which exhibits no more than 0.5 ns of edge jitter on half bit cells of exactly 1/2 BT and whose output meets the specifications of 7.4.1.1 through 7.4.1.5. This test shall be conducted in a noise-free environment. The above specified component is not to introduce more than 1 ns of edge jitter into the system.

NOTE: Special attention will have to be applied to the cable characteristics and length at 20 Mb/s.

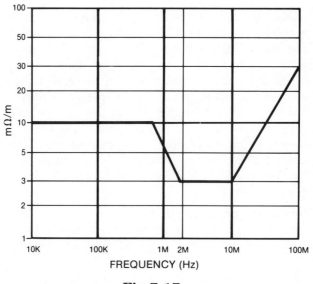

Fig 7-17
Common-Mode Transfer Impedance

7.4.3.7. Delay. Total signal delay between driver and receiver (at separate stations) for each signal pair shall not exceed 257 ns.

7.5 Functional Description of Interchange Circuits
7.5.1 General. The AUI consists of either three or four differential signal circuits, power, and ground. Two of the circuits carry encoded data and two carry encoded control information. Circuits DO (Data Out) and CO (Control Out) are sourced by the DTE, and circuits DI (Data In) and CI (Control In) are sourced by the MAU. The interface also provides for power transfer from the DTE to the MAU. The CO circuit is optional.

7.5.2 Definition of Interchange Circuits. The following circuits are defined by this specification:

Circuit	Name	Signal Direction		Remarks
		to MAU	from MAU	
DO	Data Out	X		Encoded Data
DI	Data In		X	Encoded Data
CO	Control Out	X		Encoded Control
CI	Control In		X	Encoded Control
VP	Voltage Plus	X		12 Volts
V_C	Voltage Common	X		Return for VP
PG	Protective Ground	X		Shield

7.5.2.1 Circuit DO — Data Out. The Data Out (DO) circuit is sourced by the DTE. It is a differential pair consisting of DO-A (Data Out circuit A) and DO-B (Data Out circuit B).

The signal transferred over this circuit is Manchester encoded. An *output* message containing a zero bit is encoded as CD0. An *output* message containing a one bit is encoded as CD1. An *output_idle* message is encoded as an IDL.

The following symmetry requirements shall be met when the DTE transfers pseudorandom Manchester encoded binary data over a DO circuit loaded by the test load specified in 7.4.1.1.

Bit cells generated internal to the DTE are required to be 1 BT within the permitted tolerance on data rate specified in 7.3.2. Half-bit cells in each data bit are to be exactly ½ BT (that is, the reference point for edge jitter measurements) within the permitted tolerance on the data rate specified in 7.3.2. Each transition on the DO circuit is permitted to exhibit edge jitter not to exceed 0.5 ns in each direction. This means that any transition may occur up to 0.5 ns earlier or later than this transition would have occurred had no edge jitter occurred on this signal.

7.5.2.2 Circuit DI — Data In. The Data In (DI) circuit is sourced by the MAU. It is a differential pair consisting of DI-A (Data In circuit A) and DI-B (Data In circuit B).

The signal transferred over this circuit is Manchester encoded. An *input* message containing a zero bit is encoded as CD0. An *input* message containing a one bit is encoded as CD1. An *input_idle* message is encoded as an IDL.

A DTE meeting this specification shall be able to receive, on the DI circuit without a detectable FCS error, normal preamble data arranged in legal length packets as sent by another station to the DTE. The test generator for the data on the DI circuit shall meet the requirements for drivers in MAUs specified in 7.4.1.1 through 7.4.1.5 and shall drive the DI circuit through a zero length AUI cable. Random amounts of edge jitter from 0 to 12 ns on either side of each transition shall be added by the test generator to transitions in bits in the preamble, and random amounts of edge jitter of from 0 to 18 ns on either side of each transition shall be added to the transitions in all bits in the frame. Preamble length from the test generator shall be 47 bits of preamble, followed by the 8 bit SFD.

NOTE: A significant portion of the system jitter may be non-random in nature and consists of a steady state shift of the mid-bit transitions in either direction from their nominal placement. A 16.5 ns edge jitter is expected on the transmitted signal at the receiving DTE, worst case. The difference between 16.5 ns and 18 ns jitter represents receiver design margin.

7.5.2.3 Circuit CO — Control Out (Optional). The Control Out (CO) circuit is sourced by the DTE. It is a differential pair consisting of CO-A (Control Out circuit A) and CO-B (Control Out circuit B).

The signal transferred over this circuit is encoded as described in 7.4.1.2. A *mau_request* message is encoded as CS1. A *normal* message is encoded as IDL. An *isolate* message is encoded as CS0.

7.5.2.4 Circuit CI — Control In. The Control In (CI) circuit is sourced by the MAU. It is a differential pair consisting of CI-A (Control In circuit A) and CI-B (Control In circuit B).

The signal transferred over this circuit is encoded as described in 7.3.1.2. A *mau_available* message is encoded as IDL. A *mau_not_available* message is encoded as CS1. A *signal_quality_error* message is encoded as a CS0.

7.5.2.5 Circuit VP — Voltage Plus. The Voltage Plus (VP) circuit is an optional circuit that may be sourced from the DTE. If this circuit is sourced from the DTE it shall be capable of operating at one fixed level between + 12 V dc – 6% and + 15 V dc + 5% with respect to circuit V_C for all current from 0 to 500 mA. The source shall provide protection for this circuit against an overload condition. The method of overload protection is not specified; however, under no conditions of operation, either normal or overload, shall the source apply a voltage to circuit VP of less than 0 or greater than + 15.75 V dc as specified above. MAU designers are cautioned that protection means employed by power sources may cause the voltage at signal VP to drop below the minimum operational voltage specified without going completely to zero volts when loads drawing in excess of the current supplied are applied between VP and V_C. Adequate provisions shall be made to ensure that such a condition does not cause the MAU to disrupt the medium.

If the DTE does not support circuit VP, it shall have no connection to this circuit.

7.5.2.6. Circuit V_C — Voltage Common. Circuit V_C is the ground return to the power source for circuit VP, capable of sinking 2.0 A. Also, all common mode terminators for AUI circuits shall be made to circuit V_C.

7.5.2.7 Circuit PG — Protective Ground. Circuit PG shall be connected to chassis ground through a maximum dc resistance of 20 mΩ at the DTE end.

7.5.2.8 Circuit Shield Terminations. Individual pin terminations shall meet the following requirements:
   (1) Pins 1,4,8,11,14 connected to logic ground in the DTE
   (2) Pins 1,4,8,11,14 capacitively coupled to V_C in MAU
   (3) Impedance to ground < 5 Ω at the lowest operational BR/2 in the MAU and at the highest BR in the DTE

7.6 Mechanical Characteristics
   7.6.1 Definition of Mechanical Interface. All connectors used shall be as specified in 7.6.2. The DTE shall have a female connector and the MAU shall have a male connector. The MAU may be plugged directly into the DTE or may be connected by one or more cable segments whose total length is ≤ 50 m. All cable segments shall have a male connector on one end and a female connector on the other end. All female connectors shall have the slide latch, and all male connectors shall have the locking posts (as defined in Figs 7-18, 7-19, and 7-20) as the retention system.

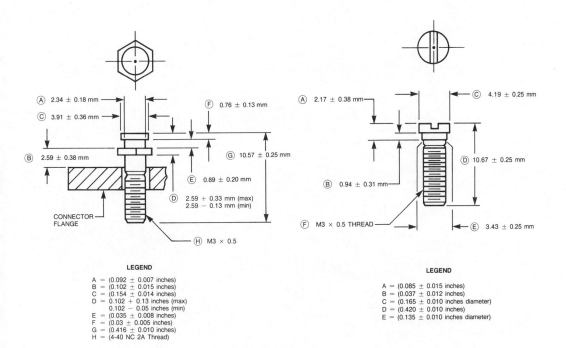

LEGEND

A = (0.092 ± 0.007 inches)
B = (0.102 ± 0.015 inches)
C = (0.154 ± 0.014 inches)
D = 0.102 + 0.13 inches (max)
   0.102 − 0.05 inches (min)
E = (0.035 ± 0.008 inches)
F = (0.03 ± 0.005 inches)
G = (0.416 ± 0.010 inches)
H = (4-40 NC 2A Thread)

LOCKING POST

LEGEND

A = (0.085 ± 0.015 inches)
B = (0.037 ± 0.012 inches)
C = (0.165 ± 0.010 inches diameter)
D = (0.420 ± 0.010 inches)
E = (0.135 ± 0.010 inches diameter)

SLIDE LATCH SCREW

Fig 7-18
Connector Locking Posts

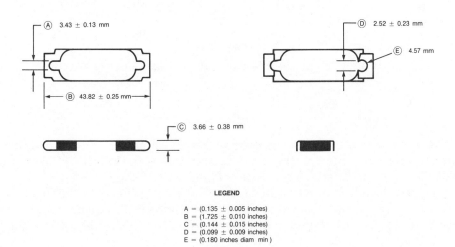

LEGEND

A = (0.135 ± 0.005 inches)
B = (1.725 ± 0.010 inches)
C = (0.144 ± 0.015 inches)
D = (0.099 ± 0.009 inches)
E = (0.180 inches diam min)

Fig 7-19
Connector Slide Latch
(material 24 gauge maximum)

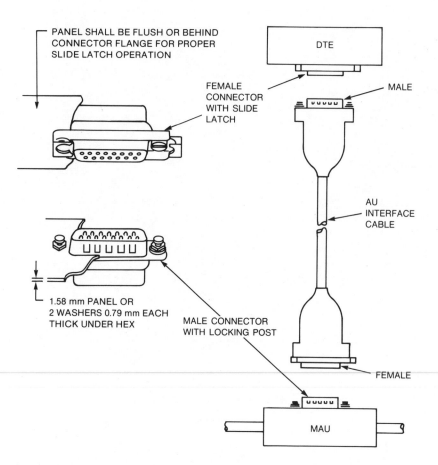

Fig 7-20
Connector Hardware and AUI Cable Configuration

7.6.2 Line Interface Connector. A 15-pin connector having the interface dimensions as specified in the common standard MIL-C-24308-1972[6] shall be used for the line interface connector. The shells of these connectors shall be plated with conductive material to insure the integrity of the cable shield to chassis current path. The resistance of the cable shield to equipment chassis shall not exceed 5 milliohms, after a minimum of 500 cycles of mating and unmating.

In order to ensure interchangeability of the mating interface connectors when obtained from different manufacturers, the female half of the connector pair shall be of the MIL-C-24308A-1972[6] dimensions and configuration and will have a conductive plating. All modifications to provide for socket shell to pin shell conductivity shall be incorporated in the shell for the male half of the connector pair. There should be multiple contact points around the sides of the male front shell to provide for this shield continuity.

The connector is not specified to prevent operator contact with the shield and precautions shall be taken at installation time to insure that the installer is warned that the shield is not to be brought into contact with any hazardous voltage while being handled by operating personnel.

7.6.3 Connector Pin Assignments. The following table shows the assignment of circuits to connector pins:

Pin	Circuit	Use
3	DO-A	Data Out circuit A
10	DO-B	Data Out circuit B
11	DO-S	Data Out circuit Shield
5	DI-A	Data In circuit A
12	DI-B	Data In circuit B
4	DI-S	Data In circuit Shield
7	CO-A	Control Out circuit A
15	CO-B	Control Out circuit B
8	CO-S	Control Out circuit Shield
2	CI-A	Control In circuit A
9	CI-B	Control In circuit B
1	CI-S	Control In circuit Shield
6	V_C	Voltage Common
13	VP	Voltage Plus
14	VS	Voltage Shield
Shell	PG	Protective Ground (Conductive Shell)

NOTE: Voltage Plus and Voltage Common use a single twisted pair in the AUI cable.

8. Medium Attachment Unit and Baseband Medium Specifications, Type 10BASE5

8.1 Scope

8.1.1 Overview. This standard defines the functional, electrical, and mechanical characteristics of the MAU and one specific medium for use with local networks. The relationship of this standard to the entire IEEE Local Network standards is shown in Fig 8-1. The purpose of the MAU is to provide a simple, inexpensive, and flexible means of attaching devices to the local network medium.

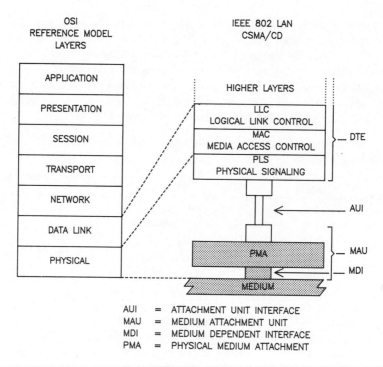

AUI = ATTACHMENT UNIT INTERFACE
MAU = MEDIUM ATTACHMENT UNIT
MDI = MEDIUM DEPENDENT INTERFACE
PMA = PHYSICAL MEDIUM ATTACHMENT

Fig 8-1
Physical Layer Partitioning, Relationship to the ISO
Open System Interconnection Reference Model

8.1.1.1 Medium Attachment Unit. The MAU has the following general characteristics:

(1) Enables coupling the PLS by way of the AUI to the explicit baseband coaxial transmission system defined in this section of the standard

(2) Supports message traffic at a data rate of 10 Mb/s (alternative data rates may be considered in future additions to the standard)

(3) Provides for driving up to 500 m (1640 ft) of coaxial trunk cable without the use of a repeater

(4) Permits the DTE to test the MAU and the medium itself

(5) Supports system configurations using the CSMA/CD access mechanism defined with baseband signaling

(6) Supports a bus topology interconnection means

8.1.1.2 Repeater Unit. The repeater unit is used to extend the physical system topology, has the same general characteristics as defined in 8.1.1.1, and provides for coupling together two or more 500 m (1640 ft) coaxial trunk cable segments. Multiple repeater units are permitted within a single system to provide a maximum trunk cable connection path of 2.5 km (8200 ft) between any two MAUs.

8.1.2 Definitions. This section defines the specialized terminology applicable to MAUs and repeater units.

Attachment Unit Interface (AUI). The cable, connectors, and transmission circuitry used to interconnect the PLS and MAU.

baseband coaxial system. A system whereby information is directly encoded and impressed on the coaxial transmission medium. At any point on the medium, only one information signal at a time can be present without disruption (see collision).

BR. The rate of data throughput (bit-rate) on the trunk coaxial medium expressed in hertz.

BR/2. One half of the BR in hertz.

branch cable. The AUI cable interconnecting the DTE and MAU system components.

carrier sense. The signal provided by the physical layer to the access sublayer to indicate that one or more stations are currently transmitting on the trunk coaxial cable.

coaxial cable. A two-conductor (center conductor, shield system), concentric, constant impedance transmission line used as the trunk medium in the baseband system.

coaxial cable interface. The electrical and mechanical interface to the shared coaxial cable medium either contained within or connected to the MAU. Also known as MDI (medium dependent interface).

coaxial cable segment. A length of coaxial cable made up from one or more coaxial cable sections and coaxial connectors, and terminated at each end in its characteristic impedance.

collision. Multiple concurrent transmissions on the coaxial cable resulting in garbled data.

collision presence. A signal provided by the physical layer to the media access sublayer (within the data link layer) to indicate that multiple stations are contending for access to the transmission medium.

compatibility interfaces. The MDI coaxial cable interface and the AUI branch cable interface, the two points at which hardware compatibility is defined to allow connection of independently designed and manufactured components to the baseband transmission system.

Medium Attachment Unit (MAU). The portion of the physical layer between the MDI and AUI that interconnects the trunk coaxial cable to the branch cable and contains the electronics which send, receive, and manage the encoded signals impressed on, and recovered from, the trunk coaxial cable.

Medium Dependent Interface (MDI). The mechanical and electrical interface between the trunk cable medium and the MAU.

Physical Medium Attachment (PMA). The portion of the MAU that contains the functional circuitry.

Physical Signaling (PLS). That portion of the physical layer, contained within the DTE that provides the logical and functional coupling between MAU and Data Link Layers.

repeater. A device used to extend the length, topology, or interconnectivity of the physical medium beyond that imposed by a single segment, up to the maximum allowable end-to-end trunk transmission line length. Repeaters perform the basic actions of restoring signal amplitude, waveform, and timing applied to normal data and collision signals.

trunk cable. The trunk coaxial cable system.

8.1.3 Application Perspective: MAU and MEDIUM Objectives. This section states the broad objectives and assumptions underlying the specifications defined throughout this section of the standard.

8.1.3.1 Object. (1) Provide the physical means for communication between local network data link entities.

NOTE: This standard covers a portion of the physical layer as defined in the OSI Reference Model and, in addition, the physical medium itself which is beyond the scope of the OSI Reference Model.

(2) Define a physical interface that can be implemented independently among different manufacturers of hardware and achieve the intended level of compatibility when interconnected in a common local network.

(3) Provide a communication channel capable of high bandwidth and low bit error rate performance. The resultant mean bit error rate, at the physical layer service interface should be less than one part in 10^8 (on the order of one part in 10^9 at the link level).

(4) Provide for ease of installation and service.

(5) Provide for high network availability (ability of a station to gain access to the medium and enable the data link connection in a timely fashion).

(6) Enable relatively low cost implementations.

8.1.3.2 Compatibility Considerations. All implementations of this baseband coaxial system shall be compatible at the MDI.

This standard provides one explicit trunk cable medium specification for the interconnection of all MAU devices. The medium itself, the functional capability of the MAU, and the AUI are defined to provide the highest possible level of compatibility among devices designed by different manufacturers. Designers are free to implement circuitry within the MAU in an application dependent manner provided the MD Interface and AUI specifications are satisfied.

Subsystems based on this specification may be implemented in several different ways provided compatibility at the medium is maintained. It is possible, for example, to design an integrated station where the MAU is contained within a physical DTE system component, thereby eliminating the AUI cable. The device designer (and system user) shall then consider such factors as topological flexibility, system availability, and configurability.

8.1.3.3 Relationship to PLS and AUI. This section defines the primary physical layer for the local area network, a layer comprised of both the physical medium and the rudimentary circuitry necessary to couple a station's message path directly to/from the medium. The complete logical physical layer of the local area network may reside physically in two distinct locations, the MAU and the DTE. Therefore, a close relationship exists between this section and Section 7. This section specifies all of the physical medium parameters, all of the PMA logical functions residing in the physical MAU, and references the AUI associated with and defined throughout Section 7.

NOTE: The design of a physical MAU component requires the use of both this section and Section 7 for the PLS and AUI specifications.

8.1.3.4 Modes of Operation. The MAU is capable of operating in either a "Normal" mode or an optional "Monitor" mode.

(1) *Normal Mode.* The MAU functions as a direct connection between the baseband medium and the DTE. Data output from the DTE is output to the coaxial trunk medium and all data on the coaxial trunk medium is input to the DTE. This mode is the "normal" mode of operation for the intended message traffic between stations.

(2) *Monitor Mode.* The MAU transmit function is disabled to prevent data from being output on the trunk coaxial medium while the receive function and collision presence function remain active for purposes of monitoring medium message traffic. This mode also serves as a limited test mode at the same time it isolates the MAU transmitter from the medium. Under most local (that is, intrastation) fault conditions the monitor mode enables continued use of the network while the local station is serviced.

8.2 MAU Functional Specifications. The MAU component provides the means by which signals on the four physically separate AUI signal circuits to/from the DTE and their associated interlayer messages are coupled to the single coaxial cable baseband signal line. To achieve this basic objective, the MAU component contains the following functional capabilities to handle message flow between the DTE and the baseband medium:

(1) *Transmit Function.* The ability to transmit serial data bit streams on the baseband medium from the local DTE entity and to one or more remote DTE entities on the same network.

(2) *Receive Function.* The ability to receive serial data bit streams over the baseband medium.

(3) *Collision Presence Function.* The ability to detect the presence of two or more stations' concurrent transmissions.

(4) *Monitor Function* (Optional). The ability to inhibit the normal transmit data stream to the medium at the same time the normal receive function and collision presence function remain operational.

(5) *Jabber Function.* The ability to automatically interrupt the transmit function and inhibit an abnormally long output data stream.

8.2.1 MAU Physical Layer Functions

8.2.1.1 Transmit Function Requirements. At the start of a frame transmission on the coaxial cable, no more than 2 bits (2 full bit cells) of information may be received from the DO circuit and not transmitted onto the coaxial medium. In addition, it is permissible for the first bit sent to contain encoded phase violations or invalid data; however, all successive bits of the frame shall be reproduced with no more than the specified amount of jitter. The 2nd bit cell transmitted onto the coaxial cable shall be carried from the DO signal line and transmitted onto the coaxial trunk cable medium with the correct timing and signal levels. The steady-state propagation delay between the DO circuit receiver input and the coaxial cable output shall not exceed one-half a bit cell. There shall be no logical signal inversions between the branch cable DO circuit and the coaxial trunk cable (for example, a "high" logic level input to the MAU shall result in the less negative current flow value on the trunk coaxial medium). A positive signal on the A signal lead of the DO circuit shall result in a more positive voltage level on the trunk coaxial medium. It is assumed that the AUI shall provide adequate protection against noise. It is recommended that the designer provide an implementation in which a minimum threshold signal is required to establish a transmit bit stream.

The Transmit Function shall output a signal on the trunk coaxial medium whose levels and waveform comply with 8.3.1.3.

In addition, when the DO circuit has gone idle after a frame is output, the MAU shall then activate the collision presence function as close to the trunk coaxial cable as possible without introducing an extraneous signal on the trunk coaxial medium. The MAU shall initiate the collision presence state within 0.6 μs to 1.6 μs after the output idle signal and shall maintain an active collision presence state for a time equivalent to 10 $\pm$ 5 bit cells.

8.2.1.2 Receive Function Requirements. The signal from the coaxial trunk cable shall be directly coupled to the receiver and subsequently ac coupled before reaching the receive circuit connected to the DTE. The receive function shall output a signal onto the DI circuit of the AUI cable which complies with the AUI specification for drivers in MAUs.

At the start of a frame reception from the coaxial cable, no more than 5 bits (five full bit cells) of information may be received from the coaxial cable and not transmitted onto the receive (DI) circuit. In addition, it is permissible for the first bit sent over the receive circuit to contain encoded phase violations or invalid data; however, all successive bits of the frame shall reproduce the incoming signal with no more than the above specified amount of jitter. This implies that the 2nd bit cell sent onto the DI circuit presents valid data to the branch cable. The steady-state propagation delay between the coaxial cable and the receive (DI) circuit output shall not exceed one half a bit cell. There are no logical signal inversions between the coaxial(trunk) cable and the MAU (branch) cable receive circuit. The circuit bandwidth of the receiver function shall be limited to 50 MHz.

A MAU meeting this specification shall exhibit edge jitter into the DI pair when terminated in the apprporite test load specified in 6.5.1.1, of no more than 8.0 ns in either direction when it is installed on the distant end of all lengths between 2.5 m and 500 m of the cable specified in 8.4.1.1 through 8.4.2.1.5 terminated at both ends with terminators meeting the impedance requirements of 8.5.2.1 and driven at one end with pseudorandom Manchester encoded binary data from a data generator which exhibits no more than 1.0 ns of edge jitter in either direction on half bit cells of exactly ½ BT and whose output meets the specifications of 8.3.1.3 except that the risetime of the signal shall be 30 ns + 0, − 2 ns. This test shall be conducted in a noise-free environment. The combination of coaxial cable and MAU receiver introduce no more than 6 ns of edge jitter into the system.

The local transmit and receive functions shall operate simultaneously while connected to the medium operating in the half duplex operating mode.

8.2.1.3 Collision Presence Function Requirements. The signal presented to the CI circuit in the absence of a collision shall be the IDL signal.

The signal presented to the CI circuit during the presence of a collision shall be the CSO signal, a periodic waveform at the nominal BR ± 15% with a duty cycle no worse than a 40/60 ratio. This signal shall be presented to the CI circuit no more than 9 bit times after the signal (for example, dc average) on the coaxial cable at the MAU equals or exceeds that produced by two (or more) MAU outputs transmitting concurrently under the condition that the MAU detecting collision presence is transmitting. Under no conditions shall the collision presence function generate an output when only one MAU is transmitting. A MAU, while not transmitting, may detect the presence of two other MAUs transmitting and shall detect the presence of more than two other MAUs transmitting. Table 1 summarizes the allowable conditions under which collisions shall be detected.

Table 1
Generation of Collision Presence Signal

MAU	Numbers of Transmitters		
	<2	=2	>2
Transmitting	N	Y	Y
Not Transmitting	N	May	Y

Y = will generate SQE message
N = will not generate SQE message
May = may generate SQE message

The collision presence function may, in some implementations, be able to sense an abnormal (for example, open) medium.

The use of MAUs in repeaters requires added considerations, see 8.3.1.5.

8.2.1.4 Monitor Function Requirements (Optional). Upon receipt of the isolate message the MAU shall, within 20 ms (implementations; solid state preferred, relay switched permitted), disable the transmit function in such a way as to both prevent the transmission of signals on the trunk coaxial medium and any abnormal loading by the disabled transmitter on the trunk coaxial medium itself. The monitor function is intended to prevent a malfunctioning active component (for example, transmit driver) from bringing down the network. The *isolate* message shall not interact with the receive or collision presence functions, thus permitting the normal operational mode wherein all data appearing on the trunk coaxial medium are carried to the DTE on the DI signal circuit.

NOTE: Verification for successful execution of the *isolate* message requires use of the trunk coaxial medium itself. This level of guaranteed performance requires use of system layers above the physical layer and implies some interruption of normal trunk coaxial medium message traffic.

8.2.1.5 Jabber Function Requirements. The MAU shall contain a self-interrupt capability to inhibit transmit data from reaching the medium. Hardware within the MAU (with no external message other than the detection of output data, bits, or leakage, by way of the transmit function) shall provide a nominal window of at least 20 ms to at most 150 ms during which time a normal data link frame may be transmitted. If the frame length exceeds this duration the jabber function shall inhibit further output data from reaching the medium.

When the transmit function has been positively disabled, the MAU shall then activate the collision presence function as close to the trunk coaxial medium as possible without introducing an extraneous signal on the trunk coaxial medium. A MAU without the monitor function and powered by the DTE may reset the jabber and collision presence functions on power reset once the error condition has been cleared. Alternatively, a self powered MAU may reset these functions after a period of 0.5 s $\pm$ 50% if the monitor function has not been implemented. If the monitor function has been implemented then it shall be used to reset the collision presence and jabber functions.

8.2.2 MAU Interface Messages

8.2.2.1 DTE Physical Layer to MAU Physical Layer Messages. The following messages can be sent by the DTE physical layer entities to the MAU physical layer entities:

Message	Circuit	Signal	Meaning
output	DO	CD1, CD0	Output information
output_idle	DO	IDL	No data to be output
normal	CO	IDL	Assume the nonintrusive state on the trunk coaxial medium
(Optional Circuit)			
isolate	CO	CSO(BR)	Positively disable the trunk coaxial medium transmitter

8.2.2.2 MAU Physical Layer to DTE Physical Layer. The following messages can be sent by the MAU physical layer entities to the DTE physical layer entities:

Message	Circuit	Signal	Meaning
input	DI	CD1, CD0	Input information
input_idle	DI	IDL	No information to be input
mau_available	CI	IDL	MAU is available for output
signal_quality_ error	CI	CSO	Error detected by MAU

8.2.2.2.1 Input Message. The MAU physical layer sends an *input* message to the DTE physical layer when the MAU has a bit of data to send to the DTE. The physical realization of the *input* message is a CD0 or CD1 sent by the MAU to the DTE on the data in circuit. The MAU sends CD0 if the input bit is a zero or CD1 if the input bit is a one. No retiming of the CD1 or CD0 signals takes place within the MAU.

8.2.2.2.2 Input Idle Message. The MAU physical layer sends an *input_idle* message to the DTE physical layer when the MAU does not have data to send to the DTE. The physical realization of the *input_idle* message is the IDL signal sent by the MAU to the DTE on the data in circuit.

8.2.2.2.3 MAU Available Message. The MAU physical layer sends the *mau_available* message to the DTE physical layer when the MAU is available for output. The *mau_available* message is always sent by a MAU that is always prepared to output data unless the *signal_quality_error* message shall be sent instead. Such a MAU does not require *mau_request* to prepare itself for data output. The physical realization of the *mau_available* message is an IDL signal sent by the MAU to the DTE on the control in circuit.

8.2.2.2.4 *Signal_Quality_Error* **Message.** The *signal_quality_error* message shall be implemented in the following fashion:

(1) The *signal_quality_error* message shall not be sent by the MAU if no MAU or only one MAU is transmitting on the trunk coaxial medium in the normal mode.

(2) If two or more remote MAUs are transmitting on the trunk coaxial medium, but the MAU connected to the local node is not transmitting, then the local MAU shall send the *signal_quality_error* message in every instance when it is possible for it to ascertain that more than one MAU is transmitting on the trunk coaxial medium. The MAU shall make the best determination possible. It is acceptable for the MAU to fail to send the *signal_quality_error* message when it is unable to conclusively determine that more than one MAU is transmitting.

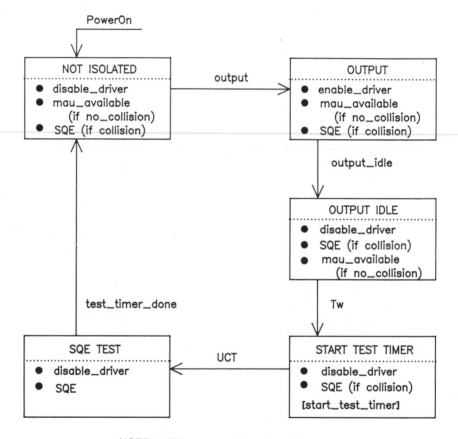

NOTE: UCT = unconditional transition
Tw = wait time, see 8.3.1.1

Fig 8-2
Interface Function: Simple MAU without Isolate Capability

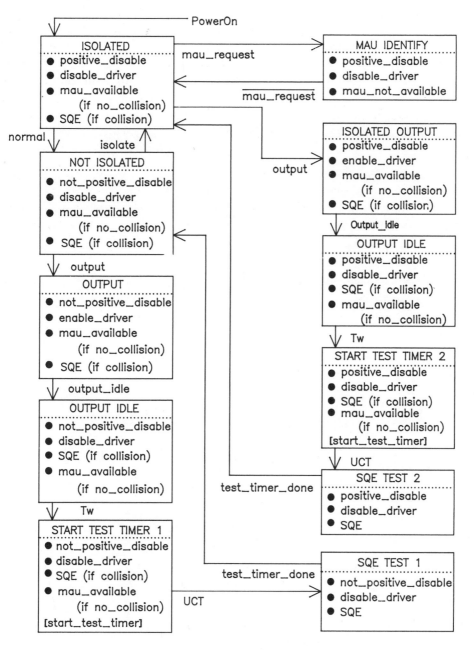

NOTE: UCT = unconditional transition
Tw = wait time, see 8.3.1.1

**Fig 8-3
Interface Function: Simple MAU with Isolate Capability**

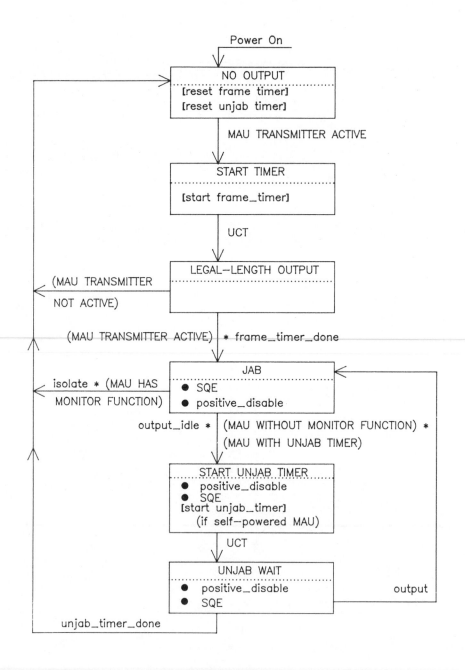

Fig 8-4
Jabber Function

(3) When the local MAU is transmitting on the trunk coaxial medium, all occurrences of one or more additional MAUs transmitting shall cause the *signal_quality_error* message to be sent by the local MAU to its DTE.

(4) When the MAU has completed each output frame it shall perform an SQE test sequence, as defined in Figs 8-2 and 8-3.

(5) When the MAU has inhibited the transmit function it shall send the *signal_quality_error* message in accordance with the jabber function requirements of 8.2.1.5.

The *signal_quality_error* message shall be asserted less than 9 bit cells after the occurrence of the multiple-transmission condition is present at the MDI and shall no longer be asserted within 20 bit cells after the indication of multiple transmissions ceases to be present at the MDI. It is to be noted that an extended delay in the removal of the *signal_quality_error* message may affect adversely the access method performance.

The physical realization of the *signal_quality_error* message is the CSO signal sent by the MAU to the DTE on the control in circuit.

Note that the MAU is required to assert the *signal_quality_error* message at the appropriate times whenever the MAU is powered and not just when the DTE is providing output data.

8.2.3 MAU State Diagrams. The state diagrams Figs 8-2, 8-3, and 8-4 depict the full set of allowed MAU state functions relative to the control circuits of the DTE-MAU interface for MAUs without conditioning requirements. Messages used in these state diagrams are explained below.

(1) *positive_disable*. Activates the positive means provided in the MAU transmitter to prevent interference with the trunk coaxial medium.

(2) *enable_driver*. Activates the path employed during normal operation to cause the MAU transmitter to impress data onto the trunk coaxial medium.

(3) *disable_driver*. Deactivates the path employed during normal operation to cause the MAU transmitter to impress data onto the trunk coaxial medium.

(4) *no_collision*. Signifies that the condition of multiple transmitters simultaneously active on the trunk coaxial medium does not exist.

(5) *collision*. Signifies that the condition of multiple transmitters simultaneously active on the trunk coaxial medium does exist.

(6) *not_positive_disable*. Deactivates the positive means provided in the MAU transmitter to prevent interference with the trunk coaxial medium.

8.3 MAU-Medium Electrical Characteristics

8.3.1 MAU-to-Coaxial Cable Interface. The following sections describe the interface between the MAU and the coaxial cable. Negative current is defined as current into the MAU (out of the center conductor of the cable).

8.3.1.1 Input Impedance. The shunt capacitance presented to the coaxial cable by the MAU circuitry (not including the means of attachment to the coaxial cable) is recommended to be no greater than 2 pF. The resistance to the coaxial cable shall be greater than 100 kΩ.

> **The total capacitive load due to MAU circuitry and the mechanical connector as specified in 8.5.3.2 shall be no greater than 4 pF.**

These conditions shall be met in the power-off and power-on, not transmitting states (over the frequencies BR/2 to BR).

The magnitude of the reflection from a MAU shall not be more than that produced by a 4 pF capacitance when measured by both a 25 ns rise time and 25 ns fall time waveform. This shall be met in both the power on and power off, not transmitting states.

8.3.1.2 Bias Current. The MAU shall draw (from the cable) between +2 μA and -25 μA in the power-off and the power-on, not transmitting states.

8.3.1.3 Coaxial Cable Signaling Levels. The signal on the coaxial cable due to a single MAU as measured at the MAU transmitter output is composed of an ac component and an offset component. Expressed in terms of current immediately adjacent to the MAU connection (just prior to splitting the current flow in each direction) the recommended signal has an offset component (direct current including the effects of timing distortion) of from -37 mA minimum to -45 mA maximum and an ac component from ± 28 mA up to the offset value. The offset component of the drive current is allowed to have relaxed values of -36 mA to -48 mA, with an ac component from ± 28 mA up to the offset value.

The current drive limit shall be met even in the presence of one or more MAU transmitters.

The MAU shall sink no more than -25 μA when the voltage on the center conductor of the cable drops to -7 V when the MAU is transmitting.

The actual current measured at a given point on the cable is a function of the transmitted current and the cable loss to the point of measurement. Negative current is defined as current out of the center conductor of the cable (into the MAU). The 10% - 90% rise fall times shall be 25 ± 5 ns at 10 Mb/s. The

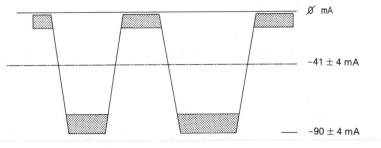

**Fig 8-5
Recommended Driver Current Signal Levels**

rise and fall times shall match within 1 ns. Figure 8-5 shows typical waveforms present on the cable. Harmonic content generated from the BR fundamental periodic input shall meet the following requirements:

2nd and 3rd harmonics: at least 20 dB below fundamental
4th and 5th harmonics: at least 30 dB below fundamental
6th and 7th harmonics: at least 40 dB below fundamental
All higher harmonics: at least 50 dB below fundamental

NOTE: Even harmonics typically are much lower.

The above specifications concerning harmonics cannot be satisfied by a square-wave with a single-pole filter, nor can they be satisfied by an output waveform generator employing linear ramps without additional waveshaping.

The signals as generated from the encoder within PLS shall appear on the coaxial cable without any inversions (see Fig 8-6).

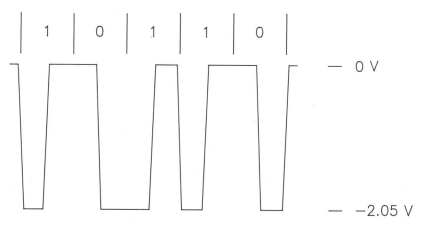

NOTES: (1) Voltages given are nominal, for a single transmitter
       (2) Rise and fall time is 25 ns nominal at 10 Mb/s rate
       (3) Voltages are measured on terminated coaxial cable adjacent to transmitting MAU
       (4) Manchester coding

Fig 8-6
Typical Coaxial Trunk Cable Signal Waveform

8.3.1.4 Transmit Output Levels Symmetry. Signals received from the AUI DI circuit shall be transmitted onto the coaxial cable with the characteristics specified in 8.3.1.3. Since the coaxial cable proceeds in two directions from the MAU, the current into the MAU is nominally twice the current measured on the coaxial cable.

The output signal of a MAU meeting this specification shall exhibit edge jitter of no more than 2.5 ns into a 25 Ω $\pm$ 1% resistor substituted for the connection to the coaxial cable when the DO circuit into the MAU is driven through a zero length AUI cable with pseudorandom Manchester encoded binary data from a data generator which exhibits no more than 0.5 ns of edge jitter on half bit cells of exactly ½ BT whose output meets the specifications of 7.4.1.1 through 7.4.1.5. The above specified component is not to introduce more than 2 ns of edge jitter into the system.

The MAU shall not transmit a negative going edge after cessation of the CD output data stream on DO or before the first edge of the next frame on the DO circuit.

8.3.1.5 Receive Collision Detect Threshold. It is recommended that the MAU implement the collision detect function with a -1.492 V to -1.629 V threshold range corresponding to the recommended tolerances for coax drive current specified in 8.3.1.3. The threshold voltage is measured on the coax at the MAU connector.

Collision detection threshold voltages tighter than those recommended above may be used to improve collision detection performance in the presence of noise on the coax, poor system component tolerances, and coax transmit levels outside of the recommended range.

A MAU that implements the recommended receive threshold shall be considered to have implemented receive mode collision detection. Receive mode collision detect indicates that a nontransmitting MAU has the capability to detection collisions when two or more MAUs are transmitting simultaneously. Repeater units require both MAUs directly connected to it to implement receive mode collision detection.[11]

8.3.2 MAU Electrical Characteristics

8.3.2.1 Electrical Isolation. The MAU must provide isolation between the AUI cable and the coaxial trunk cable. The isolation impedance measured between each conductor (including shield) of the AUI cable and either the center conductor or shield of the coaxial cable shall be greater than 250 kΩ at 60 Hz and not greater than 15 Ω between 3 MHz and 30 MHz. The breakdown of the isolation means provided shall be at least 250 V ac, rms.

8.3.2.2 Power Consumption. The current drawn by the MAU shall not exceed 0.5 A as powered by the AUI source. The MAU shall be capable of operating from all possible voltage sources as supplied by the DTE through the resistance of all permissible AUI cables. The MAU shall not disrupt the trunk coaxial medium should the DTE power source fall below the minimum operational level under abnormal MAU load conditions.

The MAU shall be labeled externally to identify the maximum value of current required by the device at any specified input voltage.

---

[11] Repeatered networks may require all MAU components to use the recommended coaxial drive connect levels. This matter is under consideration.

8.3.2.3 Reliability. The MAU shall be designed to provide an MTBF of at least 1 million hours of continuous operation without causing communication failure among other stations attached to the local network medium. Component failures within the MAU electronics should not prevent communication among other MAUs on the coaxial cable. Connectors and other passive components comprising the means of connecting the MAU to the coaxial cable shall be designed to minimize the probability of total network failure.

It should be noted that a fault condition which causes a MAU to draw in excess of 2 mA may cause communication failure among other stations.

8.3.3 MAU-DTE Electrical Characteristics. The electrical characteristics for the driver and receiver components connected to the branch cable within the MAU shall be identical to those specified in Section 7 of this standard.

8.3.4 MAU-DTE Mechanical Connection. The MAU shall be provided with a 15-pin male connector as specified in detail in the AUI specification, Section 7.

8.4. Characteristics of the Coaxial Cable. The trunk cable is of constant impedance, coaxial construction. It is terminated at each end by a terminator (see 8.5.2), and provides the transmission path for MAU device connection. Coaxial cable connectors are used to make the connection from the cable to the terminators, and between cable sections (if needed). The cable has various electrical and mechanical requirements which shall be met to ensure proper operation.

8.4.1 Coaxial Cable Electrical Parameters

8.4.1.1 Characteristic Impedance. The average characteristic cable impedance shall be $50 \pm 2 \ \Omega$, measured according to MIL-C-17-1964[5]. Periodic variations in impedance along a single piece of cable may be up to $\pm \ 3 \ \Omega$ sinusoidal, centered around the average value, with a period of less than 2 m.

NOTE: If the requirements of 7.4.2.1.1.(2), 7.4.2.1.2, 7.4.2.1.3, 7.4.2.1.4(2) are met, then it is expected that the characteristic impedance perodicity requirement shall be considered met.

8.4.1.2 Attenuation. The attenuation of a 500 m (1640 ft) cable segment shall not exceed 8.5 dB (18 dB/km) measured with a 10 MHz sine wave, nor 6.0 dB (12 dB/km) measured with a 5 MHz sine wave.

8.4.1.3 Velocity of Propagation. The minimum required velocity of propagation is 0.77 c.

8.4.1.4 Edge Jitter, Untapped Cable. Untapped coaxial cable meeting this specification shall exhibit edge jitter of no more than 8.0 ns in either direction at the receiving end when 500 m of the cable is terminated at both ends with terminators meeting the impedance requirements of 8.5.2.1 and is driven at one end with pseudorandom Manchester encoded binary data from a data generator which exhibits no more than 1.0 ns of edge jitter in either direction on half bit cells of exactly ½ BT and whose output meets the specifications of 8.3.1.3 except that the rise time of the signal shall be 30 ns + 0, – 2 ns, and no offset component in the output current is required. This test shall be conducted in a noise-free environment. The above specified component is not to introduce more than 7 ns of edge jitter into the system.

8.4.1.5 Transfer Impedance. The coaxial cable medium shall provide sufficient shielding capability to minimize its susceptibility to external noise and also to minimize the generation of interference by the medium and related signals. While the cable construction is not mandated, it is necessary to indicate a measure of performance expected from the cable component. A cable's EMC performance is determined, to a large extent, by the transfer impedance value of the cable.

The transfer impedance of the cable shall not exceed the values shown in Fig 8-7 as a function of frequency.

8.4.1.6 Cable dc Loop Resistance. The sum of the center conductor resistance plus the shield resistance, measured at 20 °C, shall not exceed 10 mΩ /m.

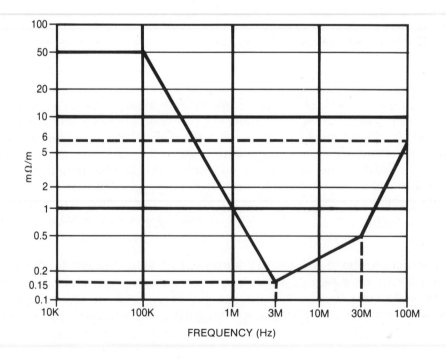

Fig 8-7
Maximum Coaxial Cable Transfer Impedance

8.4.2 Coaxial Cable Physical Parameters

8.4.2.1 Mechanical Requirements. The cable used should be suitable for routing in various environments, including but not limited to, dropped ceilings, raised floors, and cable troughs and throughout open floor space. The jacket shall provide insulation between the cable sheath and any building structural metal. Also, the cable shall be capable of accepting coaxial cable connectors, described in 8.5. The cable shall conform to the following requirements:

8.4.2.1.1 General Construction. (1) The coaxial cable shall consist of a center conductor, dielectric, shield system, and overall insulating jacket.

(2) The concentricity (for example, positional relationship between center conductor to shield system and outer jacket) of the coaxial cable elements shall be > 92% as measured in accordance with the following general configuration:

$$\frac{\text{(jacket radius)} - \text{(center offset)}}{\text{jacket radius}} \cdot 100 \geq 92\%$$

It is assumed that the offset and radius values are worst case at any point within the measured system.

(3) The coaxial cable jacket, shield system, and dielectric material shall be pierceable either by means of the connector type specified in 8.5.3.2 or by an external core tool. Overall cable system pierceability (the ability of a tap probe to pierce the jacket, shields, and dielectric cable system without substantial dielectric deformation and without causing a short circuit between center conductor and shield system) is a vital parameter affecting tap connection reliability.

Pierceability of the cable system can be measured in terms of the probe's load versus displacement signature. A pierceable cable exists where the displacement is ≥ 0.06 inches between rupture (piercing) of the shield system and contact with the center conductor.

(4) The coaxial cable shall be sufficiently flexible to support a bend radius of 254 mm (10 in).

8.4.2.1.2 Center Conductor. The center conductor shall be 2.17 mm $\pm$ 0.013 mm (0.0855 in $\pm$ .0005 in) diameter solid copper.

8.4.2.1.3 Dielectric Material. The dielectric may be of any type provided the conditions of 8.4.1.2, 8.4.1.3, and 8.4.2.1.1.3 are met.

8.4.2.1.4 Shielding System. (1) The shielding system may contain both braid and foil elements sufficient to meet the transfer impedance specifications of 8.4.1.5 and the EMC specifications of 8.7.2.

(2) The inside diameter of the innermost shield shall be 6.15 mm (0.242 in) minimum.

(3) The outside diameter of the outermost shield shall be 8.28 mm $\pm$ 0.178 mm (0.325 in $\pm$ 0.007 in).

(4) The outermost shield shall be greater than 90% coverage. The use of tinned copper braid is advised to meet the contact resistance requirements.

8.4.2.1.5 Overall Jacket. (1) Any one of several jacket materials shall be used provided the specifications of 8.4.1 and 8.4.2 are met.

(2) Either of two jacket dimensions may be used for the two broad classes of materials provided the specification of 8.4.2.1.1 are met.

(a) Polyvinyl Chloride (for example, PVC) or equivalent having an od of 10.287 mm ± 0.178 mm (0.405 in nominal ± 0.007 in).

(b) Fluoropolymer (for example, FEP, E-CTFE) or equivalent having an od of 9.525 mm ± 0.254 mm (0.375 in nominal ± 0.010 in).

The cable shall meet applicable flammability and smoke criteria and local codes for the installed environment (for example, [10]). See 8.7.4. Different types of cable sections (for example, polyvinyl chloride and fluropolymer dielectric) may be interconnected, while meeting the sectioning requirements of 8.6.

8.4.2.2 Jacket Marking. The cable jacket shall be marked with annular rings in a color contrasting with the background color of the jacket. The rings shall be spaced at 2.5 m ± 5 cm regularly along the entire length of the cable. It is permissible for the 2.5 m spacing to be interrupted at discontinuities between cable sections joined by connectors. (See 8.6.2.2 for MAU placement rules that mandate cable markings.) It is recommended that the base color of the cable jacket itself be a bright color (for example, yellow) other than that normally used for power mains.

8.4.3 Total Segment dc Loop Resistance. The sum of the center conductor, connectors, and shield resistance shall not exceed 5 Ω total per segment.

Each in-line connector pair or MAU shall be no more than 10 mΩ. Use of these components reduces the overall allowable segment length accordingly. Values given above are at 20 °C. For temperature variations, cable length shall be adjusted accordingly so that the 5 Ω total is not exceeded.

If a trunk coaxial cable segment consists of several cable sections, then all connectors and internal resistance of the shield and center conductor shall be included in the loop resistance measurement.

8.5 Coaxial Trunk Cable Connectors. The trunk coaxial medium requires termination and may be extended or partitioned into sections. Devices to be attached to the medium as MAUs require a means of connection to the medium. Two basic connector types provide the necessary connection means:

(1) Standard Type N connectors

(2) A coaxial "tap" connector

All Type N connectors shall be of the 50 Ω constant impedance type. Since the frequencies present in the transmitted data are well below UHF range (being band-limited to approximately 20 MHz), military versions of the connectors are not required (but are acceptable).

All of the coaxial tap connectors shall follow the requirements as defined in 8.5.3.

8.5.1 Inline Coaxial Extension Connector. All coaxial cables shall be terminated with the Type N plug connectors. A means shall be provided to ensure that the connector shell (which connects to the cable sheath) does not make contact with any building metal or other unintended conductor. An insulating sleeve or boot slipped over the connector at installation time is suitable.

Inline coaxial extensions between two sections of coaxial cable shall be made with a pair of Type N receptacle connectors joined together to form one "barrel". An insulating sleeve or boot shall also be provided with each barrel assembly.

8.5.2 Coaxial Cable Terminator

8.5.2.1 Termination. Coaxial cable terminators are used to provide a termination impedance for the cable equal in value to its characteristic impedance, thereby minimizing reflection from the ends of the cables. Terminators shall be packaged within an inline female receptacle connector. The termination impedance shall be 50 $\Omega \pm 1\%$ measured from 0-20 MHz, with the magnitude of the phase angle of the impedance not to exceed 5°. The terminator power rating shall be 1 W or greater.

8.5.2.2 Earthing. Either the coaxial cable terminator or inline extension connector provides a convenient location for meeting the earth grounding requirement of 8.6.2.3. It is recommended that a ground lug with current rating of at least 1500 ampacity be provided on one of the two terminators or on one extension connector used within a cable segment.

NOTES: (1) A single ground return lug on an inline connector located in the center of the cable transmission system may be used to satisfy this requirement.
(2) Alternatively, terminators might be supplied in pairs, one with and one without the ground lug connection point.

8.5.3 MAU-to-Coaxial Cable Connection. A means shall be provided to allow for attaching a MAU to the coaxial cable. The connection shall not disturb the transmission line characteristics of the cable significantly; it shall present a predictably low shunt capacitance, and therefore a negligibly short stub length. This is facilitated by the MAU being located as close to its cable connection as possible; the MAU and connector are normally considered to be one assembly. Long (greater than 30 mm) connections between the coaxial cable and the input of the MAU jeopardize this objective.

Overall system performance is dependent largely on the MAU-to-coaxial cable connection being of low shunt capacitance.

If the design of the connection is such that the coaxial cable is to be severed to install the MAU, the coaxial cable segment shall still meet the sectioning requirements of 8.6.2.1. Coaxial connectors used on a severed cable shall be type N, as specified in 8.5.1.

The type N connectors selected should be of high quality (that is, low contact resistance), to minimize the impact on system performance.

If the design of the connection is such that the piercing tap connector is to be used without severing the cable, then the tap connector and cable assembly shall conform to the mechanical and electrical requirements as defined throughout 8.5.3.1 and 8.5.3.2.

8.5.3.1 Electrical Requirements. Requirements for the coaxial tap connector are as follows:

(1) Capacitance: 2 pF nominal connector loading measured at 10 MHz

NOTE: **Total** capacitance of tap and active circuitry connected directly shall be no greater than 4 pF. Specific implementations may allocate capacitance between tap and circuitry as deemed appropriate.

(2) Contact resistance (applies to center conductor and shield contacts): 50 mΩ maximum for both shield and center conductor over useful connector lifetime

(3) Contact material: surface material on signal probe or shield sufficient to meet contact resistance requirements in environment and over time

(4) Voltage rating: 600 V dc or ac rms maximum

(5) Insulation: dc leakage resistance of tap housing shall be higher than 1 G$\cdot\Omega$ between braid and external conductors in the normal operating environment.

(6) Probe current rating: 0.1 A per contact (probe and shield)

(7) Shield current rating: 1 A surge for 1 s

8.5.3.2 Mechanical Requirements

8.5.3.2.1 Connector Housing. Shielding characteristics: > 40 dB at 50 MHz

8.5.3.2.2 Contact Reliability. Overall performance of the LAN system depends to a large extent on the reliability of the coaxial cable medium and the connection to that medium. Tap connection systems should consider the relevant electrical and mechanical parameters at the point of electrical connection between tap probe and cable center conductor to ensure that a reliable electrical contact is made and retained throughout the useful life of these components. It is recommended that some means be provided to ensure relatively constant contact loading over time, with creep, in temperature, and typical environment. Typical coaxial tap connector configurations are shown in Figs 8-7 and 8-8.

8.5.3.2.3 Shield Probe Characteristics. The shield probe shall penetrate the cable jacket and outer layer(s) of the shield system to make effective capture of the outer braid (pick 2 or more typical strands).

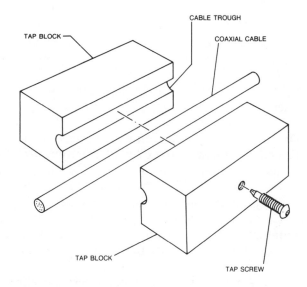

NOTE: **Tutorial only** and **not** part of specification

**Fig 8-8
Coaxial Tap Connector Configuration Concepts**

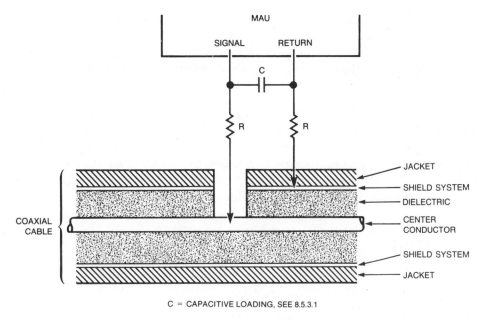

C = CAPACITIVE LOADING, SEE 8.5.3.1

R = CONTACT RESISTANCE, SEE 8.5.3.1

**Fig 8-9
Typical Coaxial Tap Connection Circuit**

8.6 System Considerations

8.6.1 Transmission System Model. Certain physical limits have been placed on the physical transmission system. These revolve around maximum cable lengths (or maximum propagation times), as these affect critical time values for the CSMA/CD access method. These maxima in terms of propagation times, were derived from the physical configuration model described here. The maximum configuration is as follows:

(1) A trunk coaxial cable, terminated in its characteristic impedance at each end, constitutes a coax segment. A coax segment may contain a maximum of 500 m of coaxial cable and a maximum of 100 MAUs. The propagation velocity of the coaxial cable is assumed to be 0.77 c minimum (c = 300 000 km/s). The maximum end-to-end propagation delay for a coax segment is 2165 ns.

(2) A point-to-point link constitutes a link segment. A link segment may contain a maximum end-to-end propagation delay of 2570 ns and shall terminate in a repeater set at each end. It is not permitted to connect stations to a link segment.

(3) Repeater sets are required for segment interconnection. Repeater sets occupy MAU positions on coax segments and count toward the maximum number of MAUs on a coax segment. Repeater sets may be located in any MAU position on a coax segment but shall only be located at the ends of a link segment.

(4) The maximum length, between driver and receivers, of an AUI cable is 50 m. The propagation velocity of the AUI cable is assumed to be 0.65 c minimum. The maximum allowable end-to-end delay for the AUI cable is 257 ns.

(5) The maximum transmission path permitted between any two stations is five segments, four repeater sets (including optional AUIs), two MAUs, and two AUIs. Of the five segments a maximum of three may be coax segments; the remainder are link segments.

NOTE: If only two link segments are used in the entire network and they are adjacent, the repeater set joining them is not required (see Fig 8-14). End-to-end jitter, propagation delay and attenuation requirements shall still be met.

The maximum transmission path consists of; 5 segments, 4 repeater sets (with AUIs), 2 MAUs, and 2 AUIs (see Fig 8-10). The total number of segments equals the number of link segments plus the number of coax segments. If

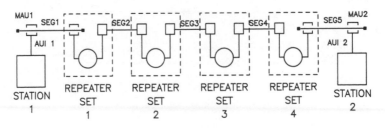

Fig 8-10
Maximum Transmission Path

there are two link segments on the transmission path, there may be a maximum of three coax segments on that path. If there are no link segments on a transmission path, there may be a maximum of three coax segments on that path given current repeater technology.

Figures 8-11, 8-12, 8-13, and 8-14 show transmission systems of various sizes

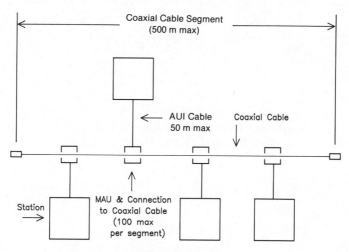

Fig 8-11
Minimal System Configuration

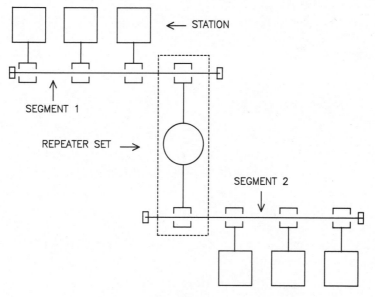

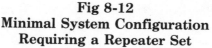

Fig 8-12
Minimal System Configuration
Requiring a Repeater Set

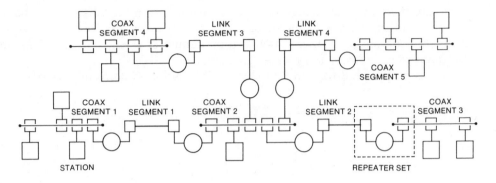

Fig 8-13
An Example of a Large System with
Maximum Transmission Paths

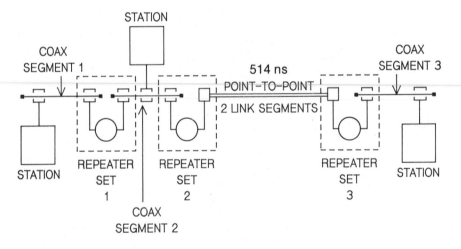

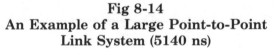

Fig 8-14
An Example of a Large Point-to-Point
Link System (5140 ns)

to illustrate the boundary conditions on topologies generated according to the specifications in this section.

8.6.2 Transmission System Requirements

8.6.2.1 Cable Sectioning. The 500 m (1640 ft) maximum length coaxial cable segment need not be made from a single, homogeneous length of cable. The boundary between two cable sections (joined by coaxial connectors; two male plugs and a barrel) represents a signal reflection point due to the impedance discontinuity caused by the batch-to-batch impedance tolerance of the cable. Since the worst-case variation from 50 Ω is 2 Ω, a possible worst-case reflection of 4% may result from the joining of two cable sections. The configuration of long cable segments (up to 500 m) from smaller sections shall be made with care. The following *recommendations* apply, and are *given in order of preference*:

(1) If possible, the total segment should be made from one homogeneous (no breaks) cable. This is feasible for short segments, and results in minimal reflections from cable impedance discontinuities.

(2) If cable segments are built up from smaller sections, it is recommended that all sections come from the same manufacturer and lot. This is equivalent to using a single cable, since the cable discontinuities are due to extruder limitations, and not extruder-to-extruder tolerances. There are no restrictions in cable sectioning if this method is used. However, if a cable section in such a system is later replaced, it shall be replaced either with another cable from the same manufacturer and lot, or with one of the standard lengths described below.

(3) If uncontrolled cable sections shall be used in building up a longer segment, the lengths should be chosen so that reflections, when they occur, do not have a high probability of adding in phase. This can be accomplished by using lengths that are odd integral multiples of a half wavelength in the cable at 5 MHz; this corresponds to using lengths of 23.4 m, 70.2 m, and 117 m (± 0.5 m) for all sections. These are considered to be the standard lengths for all cable sections. Using these lengths exclusively, any mix or match of cable sections may be used to build up a 500 m segment without incurring excessive reflections.

NOTE: If cable segments are to be added to existing installations, then care shall be taken (explicit physical or TDR measurements) to ensure that no more than a 500 m cable segment results.

(4) As a last resort, an arbitrary configuration of cable sections may be employed, if it has been confirmed by analysis or measurement that the worst-case signal reflection due to the impedance discontinuities at any point on the cable does not exceed 7% of the incident wave when driven by a MAU meeting these specifications.

8.6.2.2 MAU Placement. MAU components and their associated connections to the cable cause signal reflections due to their noninfinite bridging impedance. While this impedance shall be implemented as specified in Section 7, placement of MAUs along the coaxial cable shall also be controlled to ensure that reflections from the MAU do not add in phase to a significant degree.

Coaxial cables marked as specified in 8.4.2.2 have marks at regular 2.5 m spacing; a MAU shall only be placed at a mark on the cable. This guarantees both a minimum spacing between MAUs of 2.5 m, and controlling the relative spacing of MAUs to ensure nonalignment on fractional wavelength boundaries.

The total number of MAUs on a cable segment shall not exceed 100.

8.6.2.3 Trunk Cable System Grounding. The **shield conductor** of each coaxial cable segment **shall make electrical contact with an effective earth reference** (see ANSI/NFPA 70-1984[3], Articles 250 and 800) **at one point and shall not make electrical contact with earth elsewhere** on such objects as building structural metal, ducting, plumbing fixture, or other unintended conductor. Insulators may be used to cover any coaxial connectors used to join cable sections and terminators, to ensure that this requirement is met. A sleeve or boot attached at installation time is acceptable.

This specification is intended for use within (intraplant) buildings. Applications requiring interplant connections by way of external (outdoors) means may require special consideration beyond the scope of the standard.

The sheath conductor of the AUI cable shall be connected to the earth reference or chassis of the DTE.

8.6.3 Labeling. It is recommended that each MAU (and supporting documentation) be labeled in a manner visible to the user with at least these parameters

(1) Data rate capability in Mb/s
(2) Power level in terms of maximum current drain
(3) Safety warning (for example, shock hazard)

8.7 Environmental Specifications

8.7.1 Safety Requirements. This section sets forth a number of recommendations and guidelines related to safety concerns, the list is neither complete nor does it address all possible safety issues. The designer is urged to consult the relevant local, national, and international safety regulations to ensure compliance with the appropriate standards. EIA CB 8-1981[4] provides additional guidance on many relevant regulatory requirements.

Local area network trunk cable systems as described in this standard are subject to at least four direct electrical safety hazards during their use. These hazards are

(1) Direct contact between local network components and power or lighting circuits
(2) Static charge build-up on local network cables and components
(3) High-energy transients coupled onto the local network cabling system
(4) Potential differences between safety grounds to which various network components are connected

These electrical safety hazards, to which all similar cabling systems are subject, should be alleviated for a local network to perform properly. In addition to provisions for properly handling these faults in an operational system, special measures shall be taken to ensure that the intended safety features are not negated during installation of a new network, or during modification of an existing network.

Proper implementation of the following provisions will greatly decrease the likelihood of shock hazards to persons installing and operating the local area network.

8.7.1.1 Installations. Sound installation practice, as defined by ANSI/NFPA 70-1984, Article 820 and applicable local codes and regulations shall be followed in every instance in which such practice is applicable.

8.7.1.2 Grounding. The shield of the trunk coaxial cable shall be effectively grounded at only one point along the length of the cable. Effectively grounded means permanently connected to earth through a ground connection of sufficiently low impedance and having sufficient ampacity to prevent the building up of voltages that may result in undue hazard to connected equipment or to persons.

8.7.1.3 Safety. All portions of the trunk cabling system that are at the same potential as the trunk cable shall be insulated by adequate means to prevent their contact by either persons or by unintended conductors or grounds. The insulation employed shall provide the same or greater dielectric resistance to current flow as the insulation required between the outermost shield of the trunk cable and the above-mentioned unintended conductors. The use of insulating boots is permitted, provided that such boots (or sleeves) are mechanically and electrically equivalent to the trunk cable outer insulation characteristics and are not removed easily (that is, they shall prevent inadvertent removal by a system operator).

The MAU shall be so designed that the provisions of 8.7.1.3 and 8.7.1.4 are not defeated if the connector affixing the AUI cable to the MAU is removed.

Portions of the trunk cabling system that may become live during the dissipation of a high-energy transient by the cabling system shall also be insulated as described in 8.7.1.3.

8.7.1.4 Breakdown Path. MAUs meeting this standard should provide a controlled breakdown path which will shunt high energy transients to an effective ground either through a separate safety ground connection or through the overall shield of the branch cable. The breakdown voltage of this controlled breakdown path shall meet the isolation requirements for the MAU specified in 8.3.2.1.

8.7.1.5 Isolation Boundary. The isolation boundary between the branch cable and trunk cable specified in 8.3.2.1 shall be maintained to properly meet the safety requirements of this standard.

WARNING: It is assumed that the DTE equipment is properly earthed and not left floating or serviced by "doubly insulated ac power distribution system". The use of floating or insulated DTEs is beyond the scope of this standard.

8.7.1.6 Installation and Maintenance Guidelines. (1) When exposing the shield of the trunk coaxial cable for any reason, care shall be exercised to ensure that the shield does not make electrical contact with any unintended conductors or grounds. Personnel performing the operation should not do so if dissipation of a high energy transient by the cabling system is likely during the time the shield is to be exposed. Personnel should not contact the shield or any grounded conductor at any time.

(2) Before breaking the trunk coaxial cable for any reason, a strap with ampacity equal to that of the shield of the coaxial cable shall be affixed to the cable shield in such a manner as to join the two pieces and to maintain continuity when the shield of the trunk cable is severed. This strap shall not be removed until after normal shield continuity has been restored.

(3) At no time should the shield of any portion of the coaxial trunk cable to which a MAU or MAUs are attached be permitted to float without an effective ground connection. If a section of floating cable is to be added to an existing cable system, the installer shall take care not to complete the circuit between the shield of the floating cable section and the grounded cable section through body contact.

(4) The installation instructions for network components shall contain language which familiarizes the installer with the cautions mentioned in the above paragraphs.

(5) Network components shall contain prominent warning labels that refer installers and service personnel to the safety notes in the installation instructions.

8.7.2 Electromagnetic Environment

8.7.2.1 Susceptibility Levels. Sources of interference from the environment include electromagnetic fields, electrostatic discharge, transient voltages between earth connections, and similar interference. Multiple sources of interference may contribute to voltage build-up between the coaxial cable and the earth connection of a DTE.

The physical channel hardware shall meet its specifications when operating in either of the following conditions:

(1) Ambient plane wave field of 2 V/m from 10 kHz through 30 MHz, 5 V/m from 30 MHz through 1 GHz

NOTE: Levels typically 1 km from broadcast stations.

(2) Interference voltage of 1 V/ns peak slope, between coaxial cable shield and DTE earth connection, for example, 15.8 V peak for a 10 MHz sine wave with a 50 Ω source resistance

MAUs meeting this standard should provide adequate rf ground return to satisfy the referenced EMC specifications.

8.7.2.2 Emission Levels. The physical MAU and trunk cable system shall comply with FCC Docket 20780-1980[8].

8.7.3 Temperature and Humidity. The MAU and associated connector/cable systems are expected to operate over a reasonable range of environmental conditions related to temperature, humidity, and physical handling such as shock and vibration. Specific requirements and values for these parameters are considered to be beyond the scope of this standard. Manufacturers are requested to indicate in the literature associated with the MAU (and on the MAU if possible) the operating environment specifications to facilitate selection, installation, and maintenance of these components. It is further recommended that such specifications be stated in standard terms as specified by EIA RS-364-1971 (R1976)[1].

8.7.4 Regulatory Requirements. The design of MAU and medium components should take into consideration ANSI/NFPA-70-1984[3], Articles 250 and 800, FCC Docket 20780-1980[8], and also Appendix A, [B1], [B2], [B3], and [B6][12] to determine applicability to local or national requirements.

9. Repeater Unit

9.1 Repeater Set and Repeater Unit Specification. The repeater concepts described throughout this section are considered to be an acceptable set of specifications for a multirepeater system. It is noted that the exact parametric values specified are subject to minor refinement.[13]

9.1.1 Basic Repeater Set Configuration. Repeater sets (see Fig 9-1) are

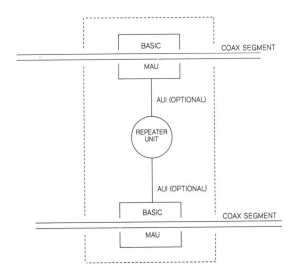

Fig 9-1
Repeater Set, Coax-to-Coax Configuration

---

[12] The numbers in brackets preceded by the letter B correspond to those of the Bibliography in Appendix A.

[13] The fundamental concepts in the section are essentially correct, however, additional statements may be needed for a complete specification. Any revision of the section may require substantial rewording in the interest of clarity and completeness.

used to extend the network length and topology beyond that which could be achieved by a single coaxial segment as defined in 8.6. If the repeater set uses discrete MAUs connected by way of AUIs to a repeater unit, the MAUs shall be Basic MAUs. A manufacturer may, if desired, integrate one or both MAUs into a single package with the repeater unit. In all cases the MAU portion of the repeater set shall be counted toward the maximum number of MAUs on each segment as specified in 8.6. A maximum of four repeater sets may be in the signal path between any two stations on the network.

9.1.2 Data Propagation

9.1.2.1 Signal Regeneration

9.1.2.1.1 Signal Amplification. The repeater set (with its associated or integral MAUs) shall ensure that the amplitude characteristics of the signals at the MAU outputs of the repeater set are within the tolerance of the specification for MAU outputs in 8.3. Therefore, loss of signal due to cable loss and noise pickup is restored at the output of the repeater set.

9.1.2.1.2 Signal Symmetry. The repeater set shall ensure that the symmetry characteristics of the signals at the MAU outputs of the repeater set are within the tolerance of the specification for MAU outputs in 8.3. Therefore, any loss of symmetry due to MAUs and cable distortion is regained at the output of the repeater set.

9.1.2.1.3 Signal Retiming. The repeater unit shall ensure that the encoded data output from the repeater unit is within the jitter tolerance of a transmitting DTE. Therefore jitter cannot accumulate over multiple segments.

9.1.2.2 Carrier Sense and Data Repeat. The repeater set shall implement the carrier sense function for both cables to which it is connected. Upon detection of carrier from one segment, the repeater set shall repeat all received signals from that segment on to the other segment.

9.1.2.3 Preamble Insertion. The repeater unit shall output at least 56 bits of preamble followed by the start frame delimiter.

9.1.2.4 Data Propagation Delays. The data propagation delay for a repeater unit is complicated by the bit insertion requirement. The data propagation delay is specified in terms of the first-bit-in to the first-bit-out and the last-bit-in to the last-bit-out.

The first-bit-in to first-bit-out delay for the repeater unit is the time between the assertion of the *input* Signal=CD on the repeated-from side to the assertion of the *output* Signal=CD on the repeated-to side. The input to output delay for the repeater unit shall be ≤ 7.5 bit times.

The last-bit-in to last-bit-out delay for the repeater unit is the time between the assertion of the *input_idle* Signal to the assertion of the *output_idle* Signal. The last-bit-in to last-bit-out delay shall be no greater than 9 bit times over the first-bit-in to first-bit-out delay without consideration of timing variations attributable to differences between input and output clocked data frequencies.

9.1.2.5 Fragment Extension. If the signal being repeated is less than 96 bits in length including preamble, the repeater unit shall extend the signal with artifical data (generated by the repeater unit) so that the total number of bits output from the repeater unit shall equal 96. The data sent to perform the extension may have any value except SFD.

9.1.3 Collision Detection and Jam Generation

9.1.3.1 Collision Presence. The repeater set shall implement the collision presence function as specified in 8.2.1.3 for both segments to which it is connected.

9.1.3.2 Jam Generation. If collision is detected on the side to which the repeater set is transmitting, the repeater set shall transmit a Jam signal to both of the segments to which it is connected. The Jam signal shall be transmitted in accordance with the repeater unit state diagram in Fig 9-2.

9.1.3.3 Collision-Jam Propagation Delays. The collision propagation delay is the period of time between the assertion of the SQE Signal and the first bit of Jam output. The SQE assert to Jam Output delay of the repeater unit shall be ≤ 6.5 bit times.

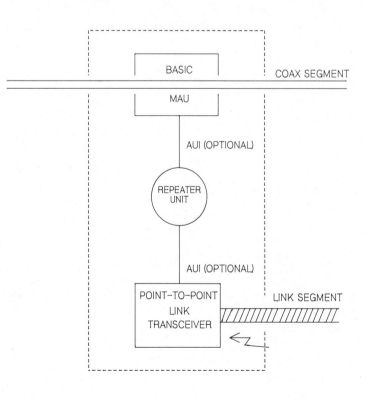

**Fig 9-2
Repeater Set, Coax-to-Link Configuration**

9.1.4 Test Functions

9.1.4.1 Jabber. The MAU functionality of the repeater set shall include the Jabber function as described in 8.2.

9.1.4.2 SQE Test. The MAU functionality of the repeater set shall include the SQE Test function as described in 8.2.

9.2 Repeater Unit State Diagram Input and Output Definitions (see Fig 9-3). The subscripts 1 and 2 are used on all the inputs and outputs of the repeater unit state diagram. The subscripts are in reference to the two

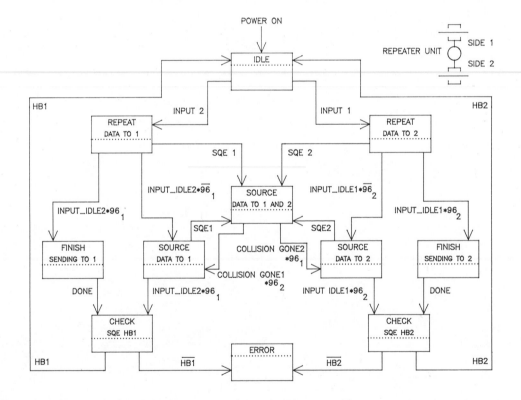

Fig 9-3
Repeater Unit State Diagram

AU Interfaces on the repeater unit. The repeater unit has two inputs designated *input_idle*; one on side 1 and one on side 2.

Signal Name	I/O	Description
input_idle	input	as specified in 7.2
input	input	as specified in 7.2
output	input	as specified in 7.2
SQE	input	Signal Quality Error as specified in 7.2
Collision_Gone	input	as specified in Fig 9-4
96	input	as specified in Fig 9-5
Done	input	signal generated internally by the repeater unit it indicates that the repeater unit has output all the bits of the repeated signal
HB	input	SQE Test pass/fail indication as specified in the Carrier Sense State Diagram in PLS HB = pass $\overline{HB}$ = fail
idle	output	output while in idle state. Used as an input by the state diagrams for Collision_Gone and 96.

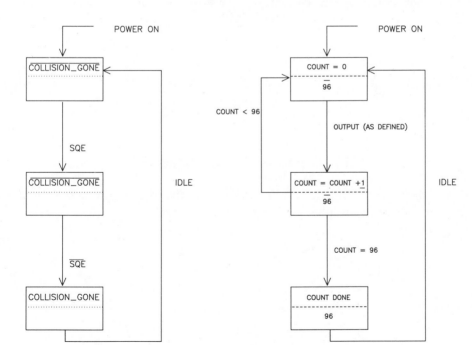

**Fig 9-4
Collision_Gone
State Diagram**

**Fig 9-5
96 State Diagram**

Table 2
Repeater Set and Repeater Unit Specification

Description	Repeater Unit	Repeater Set
input 1, 2 to *output* 2, 1	7.5 bt*	22.65 bt
input_idle 1, 2 to *output_idle* 2, 1	12.5 bt	18.65 bt
SQE to sourced *output*	6.5 bt	32.15 bt
Preamble Replacement	min = 56 bits	
input to Carrier Status_on	1.6 < x < = 3.0 bt	

*bt = bit time

10. Baseband Medium Specifications, Type 10BASE2

The elaboration of a limited distance, 10 Mb/s, low cost LAN specification is under active consideration by the CSMA/CD standard committee.

11. Broadband Specification

The elaboration of an AUI compatible broadband specification is under active consideration by the CSMA/CD standard committee.

Appendixes

(These Appendixes are not a part of IEEE Std 802.3-1985, Carrier Sense Multiple Access with Collision Detection (CSMA/CD)

Appendix A

Bibliography

References to ANSI, EIA, IEEE, MIL, and NFPA standards are not part of the equivalent ISO standard.

[B1] ANSI/UL 94-1979, Tests for Flammability of Plastic Materials for Parts in Devices and Appliances.

[B2] ANSI/UL 114-1982, Safety Standard for Office Appliances and Business Equipment.

[B3] ANSI/UL 478-1979, Safety Standard for Electronic Data-Processing Units and Systems.

[B4] DP 5525, Design Guide to Coaxial Taps. Harrisburg, PA 17105; AMP, Inc.

[B5] IEC 96-1A-1976, Supplement to IEC 96-1, Appendix Section 5.4, Terminated Triaxial Test Method for Transfer Impedance up to 1000 MHz.[14]

[B6] IEC 716-1983, Expression of the Properties of Signal Generators. (This document supersedes IEC 435-1, Safety of Data Processing Equipment, 1978.)

[B7] IS 6814, Active Tap Installation. Harrisburg, PA 17105: AMP, Inc.

---

[14] IEC Publications are available in the US from the Sales Department, American National Standards Institute, 1430 Broadway, New York, NY 10018.

Appendix B
System Guidelines

B1. Analog System Guidelines and Concepts

B1.1 Baseband Systems

B1.1.1 Overall System Objectives. The CSMA/CD Access Method, supported by baseband technology, depends on a variety of analog system components at and below the physical layer of the OSI reference model. These components provide basic interconnection facilities for the CSMA/CD access mechanism itself and are defined throughout Sections 6, 7, and 8.

Overall performance of the analog baseband medium and related physical layer capabilities depends on an optimal and known set of analog capabilities within each of these critical system elements; the coaxial trunk cable, MAUs, branch cables, DTEs, and repeater units. These system elements affect the integrity with which the serial data bit stream analog signals are carried between open systems. There are at least three critical parameters of interest: bits lost in the transmission system, signal delays, and phase jitter. It is important that these be apportioned properly among the affected system elements.

The successful interconnection of multivendor system components mandates that the values for bits lost, signal delays, and phase jitter be allocated fairly and realistically among the various system elements. The balance of Appendix B identifies the upper limits of values to be placed on the subject parameters. These values are based on the maximal system configuration (for example, four repeater units, 2.5 km trunk coaxial cable medium).

B1.1.2 Analog System Components and Parameter Values. The values given in the following table are in terms of bits and are stated as maximum values except for values given within ranges.

The initial mnemonic under each component entry refers to the system component as identified in Fig B1. System parameters are stated in terms of

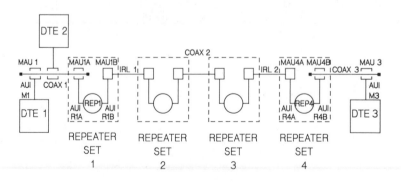

Fig B1
Maximal System Configuration Bit Budget Apportionments

the intralayer or interlayer messages sent within a station. Specific delays are called out as = delay.

The repeater concepts described through this section are considered to be an acceptable set of specifications for a multirepeater system. It is noted that the exact parametric values specified for the repeater environment are subject to minor refinement.

Component and Parameter		Start Up Delay	Last In to Last Out Delay	Start Up Loss
MEDIUM				
Trunk Coaxial Cable				
C1	Propagation	0.0	21.65	0.0
POINT TO POINT LINK				
P1	Propagation	0.0	25.64	0.0
AUI				
A1	Propagation	0.0	2.57	0.0
MEDIA ACCESS UNIT				
M1	DATA IN ASSERT -> INPUT	6.0	0.5	5.0
M2	OUTPUT -> DATA OUT ASSERT	3.0	0.5	2.0
M3	DATA IN COLLISION -> SQE ASSERT	17.0	--	--
M4	COLLISION DEASSERT -> SQE DEASSERT	20.0	--	--
M5	OUTPUT IDLE -> SQE ASSERT	$6<x<16$	--	--
M6	SQE TEST ASSERT -> SQE DEASSERT	$5<x<15$	--	--
DTE				
D1	INPUT -> INPUT UNIT	18.0	--	18.0
D2	OUTPUT UNIT -> OUTPUT	--	3.0	--
D3	INPUT -> CARRIER STATUS=CARRIER ON	3.0	--	--
D4	INPUT IDLE -> CARRIER STATUS=OFF	$3.0<x<=6.0$	--	--
D5	SQE ASSERT -> CARRIER STATUS=ON	3.0	--	--
D6	SQE DEASSERT -> CARRIER STATUS=OFF	$3.0<x<=6.0$	--	--
D7	SQE ASSERT -> SIGNAL STATUS=ERROR	3.0	--	--
D8	SQE DEASSERT -> SIGNAL STATUS=NO ERROR	$3.0<x<=6.0$	--	--
D9	CARRIER STATUS=OFF -> OUTPUT UNIT	$96<=x<=100$	--	--
D10	INPUT -> OUTPUT	8.0	--	--
D11	SIGNAL STATUS=ERROR -> JAM OUTPUT	16.0	--	--
D12	JAM OUTPUT DURATION	=32.0	--	--
REPEATER UNIT				
R1	INPUT 1,2 -> OUTPUT 2,1	7.5	--	$22<x<34$
R2	INPUT IDLE 1,2 -> OUTPUT IDLE 2,1	--	12.5	--
R3	INPUT 1,2 -> CARRIER STATUS=ON	3.0	--	--
R4	SQE -> SOURCED OUTPUT	6.5	--	--
R5	JAM OUTPUT -> OUTPUT IDLE	=96.0	--	--

Fig B1 indicates the maximal system configuration and identifies the various system component parameters considered critical in determining analog system performance.

B1.1.3 Minimum Frame Length Determination. The following table indicates the system elements that make up the minimum frame length calculation based on the worst case numbers as outlined in the bit budget of Appendix B1. The compilation in the following table is based on the following scenario:

(1) DTE 1 transmits to an adjacent DTE 2 on coax segment 1

(2) DTE 3 transmission collides with DTE 1 transmission

(3) DTE 3 is assumed to be the worst case distance from DTE 1 and its transmission just misses deferring to the DTE 1 message

(4) The collision fragment travels back down the network to inform DTE 1 that a collision has occured on its message

The frame length is constrained by two parameters:

(a) The message from DTE 1 shall be long enough so that it is still sending when the collision is detected

(b) The message from DTE 1 shall be short enough so that DTE 2 can throw out the message on the basis of being too short

Component and Function	Direction	Table Entry	Delay	Total Delay
DTE 1 STARTS TO PUT OUT FIRST BIT				0.0
DTE 1	FWD	D2	3.0	3.0
AUI M1	FWD	A1	2.57	5.57
MAU1	FWD	M2	3.0	8.6
COAX1	FWD	C1	21.65	30.2
REPEATER SET 1				
MAU 1A	FWD	M1	6.0	36.2
AUI R1A	FWD	A1	2.57	38.8
REP 1	FWD	R1	7.5	46.3
AUI R1B	FWD	A1	2.57	48.9
MAU 1B	FWD	M2	3.0	51.9
REPEATER SET TOTAL			21.64	
IRL 1	FWD	P1	25.64	77.5
REPEATER SET 2	FWD		21.6	99.1
COAX 2	FWD	C1	21.65	120.8
REPEATER SET 3	FWD		21.6	142.4
IRL 2	FWD	P1	25.64	168.1
REPEATER SET 4	FWD		21.6	189.7
COAX 3	FWD	C1	21.65	211.4
MAU 3	FWD	M1	6.0	217.4
AUI 3	FWD	A1	2.57	219.9
DTE 3 PUTS OUT A BIT	REV	D10	8.0	227.9
AUI3	REV	A1	2.57	230.5
MAU 3	REV	M2	3.0	233.5
COAX 3	REV	C1	21.65	255.1
REPEATER SET 4				
MAU 4B	REV	M3	17.0	272.1
AUI 4B	REV	A1	2.57	274.7
REP 4	REV	R4	6.5	281.2
AUI 4A	REV	A1	2.57	283.8
MAU 4A	REV	M2	3.0	286.8
REPEATER SET TOTAL	REV		31.64	

Component and Function	Direction	Table Entry	Total Delay	Delay
IRL 2	REV	P1	25.64	312.4
REPEATER SET 3	REV		31.64	344.1
COAX 2	REV	C1	21.65	365.7
REPEATER SET 2	REV		31.64	397.4
IRL 1	REV	P1	25.64	423.0
REPEATER SET 1	REV		31.64	454.6
COAX 1	REV	C1	21.65	476.3
MAU 1	REV	M3	17.0	493.3
AUI M1	REV	A1	2.57	495.9
DTE 1	REV	D7	3.0	498.9

The above table provides the scenario that enables DTE 1 to determine a collision is taking place. DTE 1 shall transmit for at least 499 bit times. To determine how much longer DTE 2 will continue to receive bits, assume that DTE 1 is the last transmitter to provide bits to the DTE 2 MAU. DTE 2 then sees:

DTE 1	FWD	D11	16.0	514.9
DTE 1	FWD	D12	32.0	547.9
AUI M1	FWD	A1	2.57	549.4

If Repeater Set 1 is the last system component to provide bits to DTE 2, then DTE 2 will see:

Component and Function	Direction	Table Entry	Total Delay	Delay
REPEATER SET 1 (1st JAM BIT)				454.6
REP 1	REV	R5	96.0	550.6
COAX 1	REV	C1	21.65	572.3

The Repeater Set is the last transmitter to provide a bit to DTE 2. The DTE 2 MAU starts seeing bits at time 8.6 which means that DTE 2 sees 563.7 bits (572.3 − 8.6). DTE 2 sees a minimum of 61 preamble bits and 8 SFD bits. The preamble and SFD bits can be deleted from the 563.7 total because they are not counted in minumum frame length.

The minimum frame length determination from the above scenario is then 564.7 − 69.0 = 494.7 bits. The 10 mbps system value for minimum frame length has been set at 512 bits.

B1.1.4 System Jitter Budgets. The typical jitter budget expected for the baseband system is apportioned in the following manner:

Encoder	0.5 nanoseconds
AUI Cable	1.0 nanoseconds (transmit end)
MAU Transmit	2.0 nanoseconds
Trunk Coax	7.0 nanoseconds
MAU Receive	-1.0 nanoseconds (with compensation)
AUI Cable	1.0 nanoseconds (receive end)
SNR on Coax	5.0 nanoseconds (SNR = 5:1)
SNR on AUI	0.5 nanoseconds (SNR = 5:1, xmit end)
SNR on AUI	0.5 nanoseconds (SNR = 5:1, rec. end)
	16.5 nanoseconds

The 18-nanosecond jitter budget leaves adequate design margin for implementation dependent considerations.

B1.1.4.1 Nominal Jitter Values. The jitter budget values given above are not expected to accommodate all step changes in phase jitter due to system parameter variations within one or a few bit times.

B1.1.4.2 Decoder Evaluation. The phase decoder in the PLS sublayer should correctly decode a Manchester encoded signal whose data transition point (center of a bit cell) has a peak-to-peak jitter of no more than 36 ns $\pm$ 18 ns deviation from the bit cell center). See Figs B2 and B3 for test method.

Evaluation of decoder performance may be simulated and tested by application of three distinct waveforms representing worst case and normal

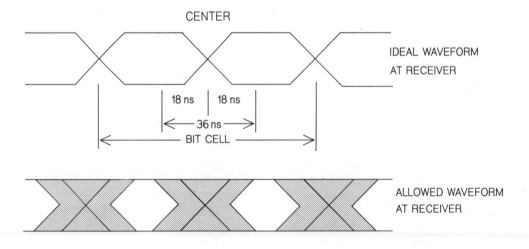

Fig B2
Typical Signal Waveforms

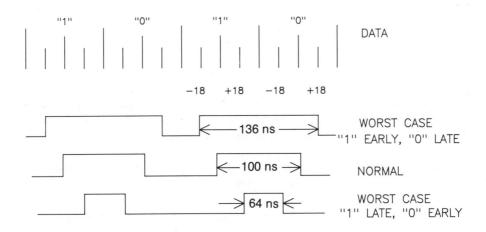

Fig B3
Worst Case Signal Waveform Variations

conditions. The waveforms contain Manchester encoded bits whose center transitions represent the extremes of maximum skew. A 5 MHz (repetition rate) pulse train whose pulse width is either 64 ns or 136 ns simulates the two worst case jitter conditions. The data output from the decoder should remain stable for each of the three test patterns and shifts between these extremes where there is a low rate of change in center transition skew. Note that the actual transmission system is not expected to permit sudden drastic changes in the steady-state edge deviation during the reception of any given frame. The above evaluation process is not intended to guarantee proper decoder performance under all operating conditions.

Appendix C
State Diagram, MAC Sublayer

C1. Introduction

This Appendix contains a generalized state machine description of the CSMA/CD procedures for MAC. It is supportive of the formal procedures defined in 4.2. It is assumed that the reader is familiar with those formal descriptions.

The state diagrams of this Appendix are descriptive rather than definitional. The formal statements of 4.2 provide the definitive specifications.

C2. CSMA/CD Media Access Control State Machine Overview

The CSMA/CD MAC consists of two components: the transmit component and the receive component. These components operate concurrently and independently.

C2.1 Transmit Component Overview. The transmit component is responsible for handling all events that affect the transmission of a frame onto the medium (see Fig C1).

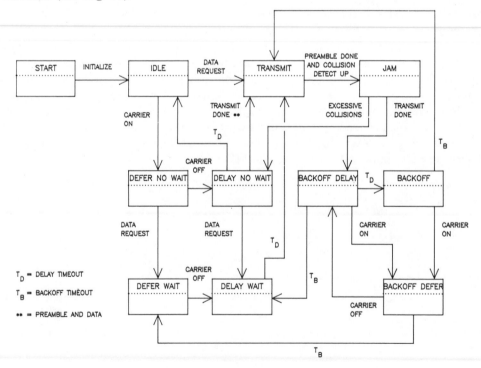

Fig C1
Transmit Component State Diagram

Table C1
Transmit Component State Transition

Current State	Event	Action	Next State
0. Start	Initialize	– Perform Initialization	Idle
1. Idle	Data Request	– Construct Frame – Start Frame Transmission	Transmit
	Carrier On	– No Action	Defer No Wait
2. Transmit	Preamble Done AND Collision Detect Up	– Start Jam Transmission – Increment Attempt Count	Jam
	Transmit Done	– Start Delay Timer – Reset Attempt Count – Indicate successful Transmission	Delay No Wait
3. Jam	Transmit Done	– Start Delay Timer – Start Backoff Timer	Backoff Delay
	Excessive Collisions	– Start Delay Timer – Indicate Transmit Excessive Collisions	Delay No Wait
4. Backoff	Carrier On	– No Action	Backoff Defer
	Back off Timeout	– Start Frame Transmission	Transmit
5. Backoff Defer	Carrier Off	– Start Delay Timer	Backoff Delay
	Backoff Timeout	– No Action	Defer Wait
6. Backoff Delay	Carrier On	– Stop Delay Timer	Backoff Defer
	Delay Timeout	– No Action	Backoff
	Backoff Timeout	– No Action	Delay Wait
7. Defer No Wait	Data Request	– Construct Frame	Defer Wait
	Carrier Off	– Start Delay Timer	Delay No Wait
8. Delay No Wait	Data Request	– Construct Frame	Delay Wait
	Delay Timeout	– No Action	Idle
9. Defer Wait	Carrier Off	– Start Delay Timer	Delay Wait
10. Delay Wait	Delay Timeout	– Start Frame Transmission	Transmit

C2.2 Transmit Component Event Descriptions

Initialize. This event is generated by management to start up the component.

Data Request. This event is generated by the LLC sublayer. It indicates there is a PDU to be transmitted.

Carrier On. This event indicates that the physical layer has detected a change in carrier sense from no carrier to carrier.

Carrier Off. This event indicates that the physcial layer has detected a change in the state of carrier sense from carrier to no carrier.

Preamble Done AND Collision Detect Up. This event indicates that the physical layer has detected a collision with the frame being transmitted and the transmission of the preamble sequence is completed.

Delay Timeout. This event indicates that the interframe time delay has completed.

Backoff Timeout. This event indicates that the time period for backing off has completed.

Transmit Done. The bit transmitter has transmitted all of the bits in the transmit buffer specified by the transmit buffersize (which includes preamble and data).

Excessive Collisions. The bit transmitter has transmitted all of the bits in the transmit buffer specified by the transmit buffersize, and the attempt count is equal to the maximum transmit attempt count allowed.

C2.3 Transmit Component Action Descriptions

Construct Frame. This action encapsulates the data field with the Preamble, SFD, DA, SA, Length, PAD and FCS fields.

Start Frame Transmission. This action initiates bit transmission of the frame.

Start Jam Transmission. This action causes the bit transmitter to transmit the bits of the jam pattern.

Indicate Successful Transmission: This action reports that the transmission was successful.

Indicate Transmit Failure. This action reports the failure of transmission and the reason.

Increment Attempt Count. This action increments the counter used to record the number of attempts made to transmit the same frame.

Reset Attempt Count. This action initializes the attempt count to 0.

Start Backoff Timer. This action computes the random backoff delay time and sets the backoff timer to that time.

Start Delay Timer. This action sets the delay timer to the interframe gap time.

Stop Delay Timer. This action turns the delay timer off.

Perform Initialization. This action turns all timers off and ensures that carrier is considered off and collision detect down. All counters are reset. Any implementation specific variables are initialized.

C2.4 Transmit Component State Descriptions

Start. The transmit component has not been initialized by management.

Idle. The transmit component is not transmitting any data nor is it in a state where it is prevented from transmitting data.

Transmit. The transmit component is actively transmitting bits onto the medium.

Jam. The transmit component is actively transmitting jam bits onto the medium.

Backoff. The transmit component is waiting for its random backoff delay to expire before attempting to retransit a frame.

Backoff Defer. The transmit component is waiting for both the medium to become available and for its backoff time delay to expire before attempting to retransmit a frame.

Backoff Delay. The transmit component is waiting for the interframe gap and the backoff delays to expire before attempting to retransmit a frame.

Defer No Wait. The transmit component has no frame to transmit and it cannot transmit one if it gets one because the medium is busy.

Delay No Wait. The transmit component has no frame to transmit and it could not if it had one because it is waiting for the interframe gap time to expire.

Defer Wait. The transit component is waiting for the medium to become free before attempting to transmit or retransmit the frame.

Delay Wait. The transmit component is waiting for the interframe gap time to expire before attempting to transmit or retransmit the frame.

C3. Receive Component Overview

The receive component is responsible for handling all events that affect the reception of a frame from the media (see Fig C2).

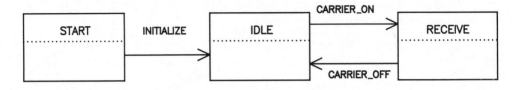

Fig C2
Receive Component State Diagram

Table C2
Receive Component State Transition

Current State	Event	Action	Next State
0. Start	Initialize	– Perform Initialization	Idle
1. Idle	Carrier On	– Start Receiving	Receive
2. Receive	Carrier Off	– Process Frame Received	Idle

C3.1 Receive Component Event Descriptions

Initialize. This event is generated by management to start up the component.

Carrier On. This event indicates that the physical layer has detected a change in carrier sense from no carrier to carrier.

Carrier Off. This event indicates that the physical layer has detected a change in the state of carrier sense from carrier to no carrier.

C3.2 Receive Component Action Descriptions

Perform Initialization. This action turns all timers off and ensures that carrier is considered off and collision detect down. All counters are reset. Any implementation specific variables are initialized.

Start Receiving. This action begins the processes of accepting bits and appending them to the buffer used to contain the frame.

Process Frame Received. If the frame is not addressed to this station then ignore the frame. Otherwise check the frame for errors. If there are no errors pass the frame up to the LLC sublayer indicating no error. Otherwise, pass the frame to the LLC sublayer indicating the error.

C3.3 Receive Component State Descriptions

Start. The receive component has not been initialized by management.

Idle. The receive component is not actively receiving bits of data from the line.

Receive. The receive component is receving bits of data from the line.

Acknowledgements

Appreciation is expressed to the following companies and organizations for contributing the time, talent, and resources of their employees to make possible the development of this text:

Ericcson Information Systems	Rockwell International
National Semiconductor, Corp	E-Systems, Inc
NCR Corp	Tektronix, Inc
Amp Inc	GTE Corp
Hewlett Packard Co	Interlan, Inc
Xerox Corp	Grumman Corp
BBN Computer Corp	National Bureau of Standards
Motorola, Inc	Codex Corp
Advanced Micro Devices, Inc	TRW Corp
3 Com Corp	AT&T Information Systems, Inc
Intel Corp	Data General Corp
Ungermann-Bass Inc	BNR, Inc
ICL PLC	IBM Corp
Olivetti Nuova	HIS Electro Mechanics, Inc.
Bridge Communications, Inc	Grid Systems Corp
Allied Corporation	General Electric Co
Siemens AG	Concord Data Systems, Inc
Digital Equipment Corp	Bell AT&T Laboratories
Malco, A. Microdot Co	Signetics Corp
Mitre Corp	RCA Automated Systems